Computer Jargon

The Illustrated Glossary of Basic Computer Terminology

Kevin Wilson

www.elluminetpress.com

Computer Jargon

About the Author

With over 20 years' experience in the computer industry, Kevin Wilson has made a career out of technology and showing others how to use it. After earning a master's degree in computer science, software engineering, and multimedia systems, Kevin has held various positions in the IT industry including graphic & web design, programming, building & managing corporate networks, and IT support.

He serves as senior writer and director at Elluminet Press Ltd, he periodically teaches computer science at college, and works as an IT trainer in England while researching for his PhD. His books have become a valuable resource among the students in England, South Africa, Canada, and in the United States.

Kevin's motto is clear: "If you can't explain something simply, then you haven't understood it well enough." To that end, he has created the Exploring Tech Computing series, in which he breaks down complex technological subjects into smaller, easy-to-follow steps that students and ordinary computer users can put into practice.

You can contact Kevin using his email address:

office@elluminetpress.com

0-9

100BaseFX is an Ethernet LAN standard that runs over fibre optic cable at 100Mbps and can carry data a maximum distance of 2km full duplex. "Base" indicates baseband signalling, and the letter "F" indicates fiber-optic cable.

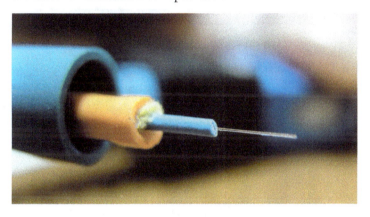

100BaseT is an Ethernet standard that runs at 100Mbps over UTP cable such as Cat5 or Cat5e, and can carry data up to 100m. "Base" indicates baseband signalling, and the letter "T" indicates twisted pair copper cabling.

1000BaseT also known as Gigabit Ethernet, is an Ethernet standard that runs at 1Gbps over UTP cable such as Cat-5e, and Cat-6. Can carry data up to 100m.

1080i is a display resolution used in HDTV with a resolution of 1920×1080 pixels and is also known as Full HD. The "i" stands for interlaced where the image is refreshed on the screen by scanning lines 1, 3, 5... on the first scan, then lines 2, 4, 6... on the second scan.

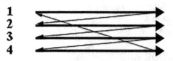

1080p is a display resolution used in HDTV with a resolution of 1920×1080 pixels and is also known as Full HD. The "p" stands for progressive scan where the image on the screen is refreshed by scanning each line in sequence.

10Base2 also known as thinnet and is a variant of Ethernet that uses thin coaxial cable terminated with BNC and T-connectors to connect computers together.

10Base5 also known as Thicknet, an early Ethernet standard that used thick coaxial cable and supported 10 Mbps over a maximum cable length of 500m.

10BaseT is an Ethernet LAN standard that runs over UTP cable and runs at 10mbps.

10GBase-T a 10 Gbps Ethernet standard that runs over twisted-pair copper cabling (Cat6, Cat6a, and Cat7) and supports distances up to 100m.

16-Bit Audio is a unit of measure that indicates the resolution of a digitised sound sample and uses 16 bits per sample. The higher the resolution, the better the audio fidelity. 16-bit audio is the standard used for standard audio Compact Discs (CD-DA)

1GL or First Generation Language is a programming language that uses nothing but binary machine code.

24p refers to 24 frames per second progressive scan. This is the frame rate of motion picture film. It is also one of the rates allowed for transmission in the DVB and ATSC television standards, allowing them to handle film without needing any frame rate change. It is now accepted as a part of television production formats, usually associated with high-definition, 1080-line, progressive scans.

2-Factor Authentication is an extra level of security included in many online services, where a confirmation code is sent to the user's cell/mobile phone number or email address that was registered when the account was opened.

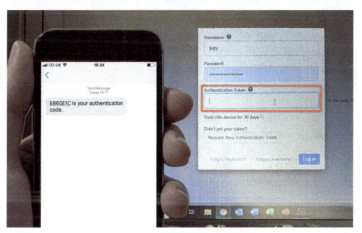

2GL or Second Generation Language is a programming language that uses assembly language mnemonics which are assembled into machine code for execution.

3D API is a 3D application programming interface that controls all aspects of the 3D rendering process such as Microsoft's DirectX and OpenGL.

3D Graphics is the display of objects and scenes in 3 dimensions: height, width, and depth. The information is calculated using 3D a co-ordinate system that represents three dimensions as x, y, and z axes.

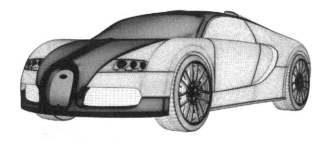

3D Sound is a blanket term for technologies that alter the way sound is distributed in real-world space. Spatialisation broadens the soundstage (the area in space where the sound seems to be coming from), making it more dramatic and spacious, and gives the illusion of pushing it beyond the physical location of the speakers. Positional audio uses encoded audio streams to position sounds realistically in the space around the listener when the sounds are played back on compatible equipment.

3G is short for Third Generation wireless mobile telecommunications technology.

3GL or Third Generation Language is a programming language that is machine independent that uses english-like statements that are compiled or interpreted for execution. Common examples are C, C++, Python, Basic and Pascal.

4G is short for Fourth Generation wireless mobile telecommunications technology, and the successor to 3G.

4GL or Fourth Generation Language uses english like statements with a minimum of programming code such as SQL.

4K also known as UltraHD (or UHD) and is a resolution used in digital televisions and monitors with a resolution of 3840×2160 pixels in many consumer displays (2160p), and 4096×2160 in digital cinema.

5G is short for Fifth Generation wireless mobile telecommunications technology, and the successor to 4G.

64-bit Computing is a computer architecture that processes 64-bit data at a time and can address much larger amounts of memory (theoretically 16 exabytes).

128-bit Encryption is a form of data encryption that uses a 128-bit key, offering a strong level of security for data protection.

256-bit Encryption is a highly secure encryption method using a 256-bit key, commonly used in AES (Advanced Encryption Standard) and VPNs.

68000 is a CISC microprocessor introduced in 1979 by Motorola and was used in the Apple Lisa and early models of Amiga, Atari ST, and Macintosh computers.

5GL or Fifth Generation Language is a programming language that is based on problem-solving and is often used in AI.

720p is a resolution used in HDTV with a resolution of 1280×720 pixels and is also known as HD Ready. The "p" stands for progressive scan where the image on the screen is refreshed by scanning each line in sequence.

802.3 is the IEEE standard for Ethernet, covering wired LAN technologies such as 10Base-T, 100Base-T, and 1000Base-T.

802.11a is a wireless networking standards that operates in the 5 GHz band with a maximum net data rate of 54 Mbps.

802.11ac is a wireless networking standards that operates in the 5 GHz band with a maximum net data rate of 500 Mbps - 6.9Gbps.

802.11ax (Wi-Fi 6 & Wi-Fi 6E) is latest Wi-Fi standard that operates on 2.4 GHz, 5 GHz, and 6 GHz (Wi-Fi 6E), with higher efficiency, lower latency, and speeds up to 9.6 Gbps.

802.11b is a wireless networking standards that operates in the 2.4 GHz band with a maximum net data rate of 11 Mbps.

802.11g is a wireless networking standards that operates in the 2.4 GHz band with a maximum net data rate of 54 Mbps.

802.11n is a wireless networking standards that operates on both 2.4 and 5 GHz band with a maximum net data rate of 54 - 600 Mbps.

802.15.4 is a wireless communication standard used in low-power, short-range networks like Zigbee and Thread (IoT applications).

8086 is a 16-bit microprocessor chip designed by Intel that gave rise to the x86 architecture. The chip had a 16-bit data bus, 20-bit external bus, 64K I/O ports and ran at up to 10Mhz.

80286 introduced in by Intel in 1982, and was a 16-bit microprocessor that significantly improved performance over its predecessor, the 8086. It introduced protected mode, allowing access to more than 1MB of RAM, which was a major limitation of real mode. The clock speeds started at 6 MHz and later models reached 25 MHz. It was widely used in the IBM PC/AT and early personal computers, but its protected mode had limitations, as switching back to real mode required a full system reset..

80386 released in 1985 and was the first 32-bit microprocessor in the x86 family, enabling multitasking and virtual memory. It supported both real mode and protected mode, making it more versatile than the 80286. The 386 introduced 32-bit registers and a 32-bit data bus, significantly improving performance. It was initially available at 12 MHz and later models reached 40 MHz. This processor was a major milestone in PC computing, as it laid the foundation for modern operating systems such as Windows and Linux.

80486 introduced in 1989 and was a 32-bit processor that built upon the 386 architecture, adding an integrated floating-point unit (FPU) and an on-chip cache. This integration greatly improved computational performance. The 486DX version included an FPU, while the 486SX was a cost-reduced model without one. Clock speeds started at 20 MHz and eventually reached 100 MHz. The 80486 was widely used in early 1990s PCs, providing a significant speed boost for applications and games. Below is a 486DX2-66 running Windows 3.1.

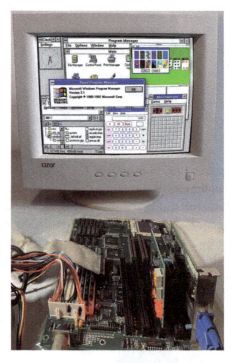

8-Bit Audio is a digital audio format where each sound sample is stored using 8 bits, allowing for 256 discrete amplitude levels. While lower in fidelity than 16-bit or 24-bit audio, it was commonly used in early computers, video game consoles, and synthesizers due to its small file size and simpler processing requirements.

AAAA Record is a record on a DNS server that maps a domain name to an IPv6 address.

A Record is a record on a DNS server that maps a domain name to the IPv4 address.

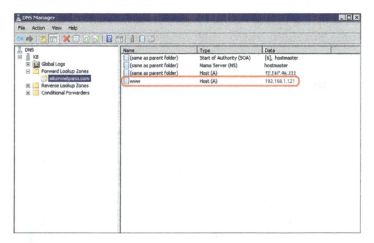

A3D is a positional audio technology and audio API developed by Aureal Semiconductor Inc. A3D provides a real-life audio experience by surrounding the listener with sounds in 3D using only a single pair of ordinary speakers or headphones.

Abort is to terminate or stop a computer program from running usually when there is an error.

AC stands for Alternating Current and is the electricity generated at a power plant and distributed to homes and offices. The voltage is 110v in the US and 250v in the UK. Alternating means the direction of the current is reversed 60 times a second (60Hz) in the US and 50 times a second (50Hz) in the UK.

AC 97 is an audio codec standard developed by Intel in 1997 used on PC motherboards and sound cards to supply audio to the system.

Access Control List is a list of permissions that specify what operations a user can perform on a resource such as a shared resource, folder or file.

Access Time is the time taken between the requested for data from memory or a peripheral device, and the moment the information is returned. Access time includes the actual seek time, rotational latency, and command processing overhead time.

Accumulator is a register in the CPU used to temporarily store the result of a calculation during the execution of an instruction.

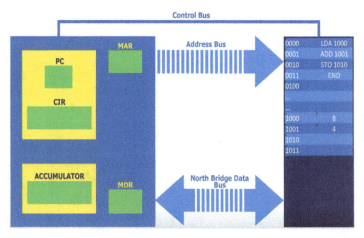

ACK short for acknowledgement, a notification sent from one network device to another to acknowledge an event or receipt of a message.

ACPI stands for Advanced Configuration and Power Interface and is an interface for controlling power management and monitoring the health of the computer system.

ACR stands for Advanced Communication Riser, a rival riser card architecture to Intel's CNR specification, which emerged at about the same time and offers similar features.

Acrobat is an Adobe application for producing documents that can either be printed or displayed on the screen, with the correct fonts and layout on a variety of different devices and operating systems. Usually a PDF document.

Action Center is a slideout panel included in Windows 10 that displays notifications from various apps, system events, and provides quick access toggles to various settings.

Active Directory is a directory service usually running on a server called a domain controller and is found on Microsoft Domain Networks. The active directory contains registered user accounts, as well as any available services and resources such as printers, etc

Active Matrix is an LCD technology used in flat panel monitors and televisions that produces a brighter and sharper display with a broader viewing angle than passive matrix screens. Active matrix technology uses a thin film transistor at each pixel and is often designated as a TFT screen. See also Passive Matrix.

ActiveX is a deprecated technology developed by Microsoft. Introduced in 1996, ActiveX components (or controls) were embedded in web pages to extend functionality and interactivity. Most modern browsers no longer support ActiveX.

Actuator is the internal mechanism of a hard disk drive that moves the read/write head to the correct track on the surface of the disk. The actuator itself, typically consists of a rotary voice coil and a series of arms. At the end of each arm is a read/write head. As a voltage is applied to the voice coil, it rotates, positioning the heads over the desired track on the surface of the disk.

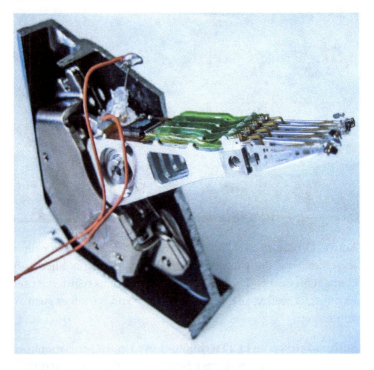

Adaptive Compression is data compression software that continually changes its compression algorithm depending on the type and content of the data being compressed.

ADC is short for analogue to digital converter and is a device that converts continuously varying analogue signals into binary code for the computer. The converter may be contained on a single chip or can be one circuit within a chip.

ADD2 is a PCI Express card that can be used to display system output on a television, digital display, or simultaneously to a monitor and digital display.

Adder or Full Adder is a digital circuit that is used in the arithmetic logic unit of a CPU to add two numbers.

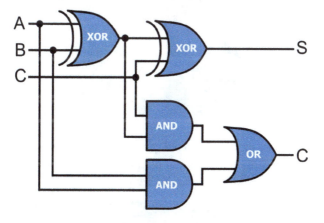

A and B are the two numbers being added together, C is the carry. The truth table would be:

Input			Output	
A	**B**	**CARRY**	**SUM**	**CARRY**
0	0	0	0	0
0	0	1	1	0
0	1	0	1	0
0	1	1	0	1
1	0	0	1	0
1	0	1	0	1
1	1	0	0	1
1	1	1	1	1

Additive

Additive Colour also known as RGB colour. Additive colours are created by mixing different amounts of light using the three primary colours: red, green, and blue. Additive colour mixing begins with black and ends with white, meaning that as more colour is added, the result is lighter and more white. TVs, projectors and computer monitors use the additive colour to create images on screen.

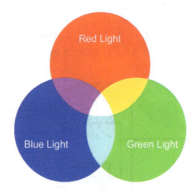

Address is a unique reference point to a memory location, a location on a storage device, or peripheral device. This is known as an absolute address or real address.

Relative address is an address expressed as an offset from the value of a register such as the program counter (PC), or the distance from a base address.

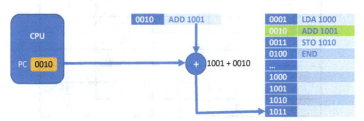

Address Bus is the channel between the CPU and the main memory (RAM) and I/O devices, that allows the CPU to send an address.

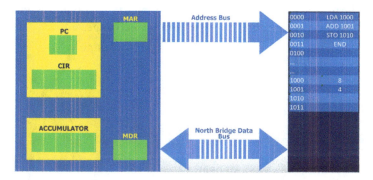

Address Space is the total amount of memory addresses the address bus can contain.

Addressability refers to how many pixels can be sent to the display horizontally and vertically. The most common combinations currently in use are 640×480 (VGA mode), 800×600 (SVGA mode), 1024×768, 1280×1024 and 1600×1200.

Administrator is a user account often created when the operating system is installed that allows full access to the system.

Administrator Tools are specialised utilities and programs used for backup, monitoring, error checking, troubleshooting and system management.

ADSL stands for Asymmetrical Digital Subscriber Line, and is a data communications technology provided over copper telephone lines. With ADSL, the download speed is greater than the upload speed, hence the name asymmetric. Max transmission speed depends on the distance from the exchange.

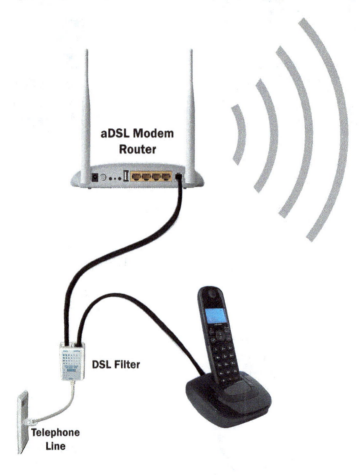

aDSL Modem
Router

DSL Filter

Telephone
Line

Adware is a program that tracks your activity across different websites and generates targeted adverts and popups usually to the annoyance of the user.

AGP stands for Accelerated Graphics Port and is a 32-bit PC bus architecture introduced in 1997 allowing graphics cards direct access to the system bus, rather than going through the slower PCI bus. AGP was phased out in favour of PCI-Express.

AHCI stands for Advanced Host Controller Interface defined by Intel that provides a standard interface that enables software to communicate with a SATA device such as a hard disk drive using advanced SATA features such as native command queuing (NCQ), hot swapping and power management.

AI See Artificial Intelligence.

Ajax (Asynchronous JavaScript and XML) is a web development technology that allows web pages to communicate with a web server asynchronously, enabling dynamic and interactive user experiences without requiring the entire page to be reloaded. Ajax enables web applications to retrieve data from the server, send data, and update specific parts of a web page asynchronously in the background, without interrupting the user's interaction with the application. Ajax combines JavaScript, XML (or other data formats such as JSON), and asynchronous HTTP requests to exchange data between the client and server, facilitating responsive and interactive web applications.

AIFF stands for Audio Interchange File Format and is used for high end audio applications.

Algorithm is a sequence of instructions a computer uses to perform a task. An example could be a search algorithm that searches a database for a given term, or a sort algorithm that sorts a list into alphabetical order.

Aliasing is a form of image distortion associated with signal sampling. A common form of aliasing is a stair-stepped appearance along diagonal and curved lines. Another is moiré, two geometrically regular patterns such as two sets of parallel lines or two halftone screens superimposed.

Alpha is an additional colour component along with red, green, and blue (RGB) channels often used to denote transparency or opacity.

Alpha Blending is a technique in computer graphics used to combine two or more images or colors based on their alpha values (transparency levels). It allows for smooth transitions, semi-transparent effects, and realistic overlays by determining how much of each image contributes to the final visual output.

Alpha Channel is the component of an image that is used to determine the transparency or opacity of a colour and is usually expressed as a percentage. Full transparency is 0% and full opacity is 100%.

ALT GR or ALT Graph Key is a modifier key on a keyboard often used to insert special characters, or international characters such as currency, accent letters or special typographic marks.

For example.

```
AltGr 4 = €
AltGr R = ®
AltGr C = ©
AltGr T = ™
```

ALT Key is a modifier key on a keyboard often used in keyboard shortcuts.

ALU is short for Arithmetic and Logic Unit: the part of a CPU that performs arithmetic commands such as addition, subtraction, multiplication and division, as well as logic commands such as OR, AND, or NOT.

AM is short for Amplitude Modulation and is a data transmission technique that encodes the data by varying (or modulating) the amplitude of the carrier wave.

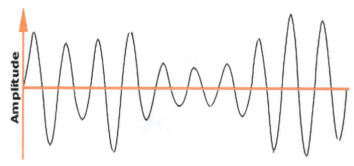

Ambient Light Sensor is an optical sensor that detects the amount of ambient light in an environment. Ambient light sensors are often found in laptops, tablets and mobile phones allowing the device to automatically control the screen's brightness

Analogue is a signal or data that is represented by a continuously varying physical quantity such as a voltage. The signal is subject to interference from an electromagnetic source.

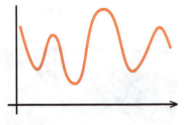

Analogue Video is a video that is represented by an analogue signal which also includes luminance, brightness (Y) and chrominance (U & V). See analogue and digital.

Anamorphic means unequally scaled in vertical and horizontal dimensions. Footage is shot with an anamorphic lens and appears squashed when captured but is correct when played back. In this way, the footage can be formatted with varying aspect ratios such as 16:9 or 4:3

AND Gate has two inputs. AND gates require both inputs to be 1 for the output to be 1. Expressed as `Out = A.B`

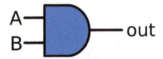

The truth table would be

A	B	Output
0	0	0
0	1	0
1	0	0
1	1	1

Android an open source mobile operating system based on a modified linux kernel found on touchscreen smartphones and tablets.

Animated GIF is a file containing a series of images commonly used on websites for short animated effects

Anode in a cathode ray tube (CRT) and electrolysis is the positively charged electrode . In a battery the anode is the negative terminal as it's the part of the battery that releases electrons into the external circuit, providing electric current to power devices.

ANSI is short for American National Standards Institute. A standards-setting, non-government organisation which develops and publishes standards for voluntary use in the United States.

Anti-aliasing is the process of smoothing out the jagged edges of bitmapped images by modulating the intensity on either side of the edge boundaries creating blurring which reduces the jagged appearance.

Anit-malware is a software utility, such as malwarebytes, designed to remove malicious programs from a computer and to prevent them from damaging a computer or data.

Apache a free open-source cross-platform web server software that powers various web servers on the internet, and is actively maintained by the Apache Software Foundation. Apache usually runs on a linux distribution but can also run on windows.

Aperture Grille is used in certain CRT displays, particularly Trinitron monitors and televisions, to enhance image sharpness and color accuracy. It consists of a vertical array of fine wires that replace the traditional shadow mask, allowing more electrons to pass through and improving brightness and clarity..

API is short for Application Programming Interface and is a set of functions that an application can call to perform a task. APIs allow one application to communicate with other applications and services without having to know how they're written. For example, if you're using a Windows application such as Word, and you want to save a file, Word will call the save dialog box function from the Windows API.

APM stands for Advanced Power Management and is an API that allows an OS to communicate with the computer's BIOS to reduce power consumption by throttling components or turning them off.

App is a software application often found on tablets and smartphones. Apps are usually smaller than applications and are designed to take advantage of touch screens on mobile devices

Applet is a small program that performs a limited range of tasks such as a Java applet.

Application is a piece of software or computer program written to perform a task such as Microsoft Word and Adobe Photoshop.

Application Layer is the topmost layer in the OSI (Open Systems Interconnection) model and the TCP/IP (Transmission Control Protocol/Internet Protocol) protocol stack, representing the interface between software applications and the underlying network infrastructure. The Application Layer provides communication services and protocols that enable applications to exchange data over a network, regardless of the underlying hardware or network technologies. Examples of protocols and services at the Application Layer include HTTP (Hypertext Transfer Protocol) for web browsing, SMTP (Simple Mail Transfer Protocol) for email, FTP (File Transfer Protocol) for file transfer, and DNS (Domain Name System) for domain name resolution.

Architecture is a specification that describes how hardware and software technologies are designed and how they interact to form a computer system or platform such as the Von Neumann architecture.

Archive is to copy applications or data onto a storage medium for long-term storage of data.

Argument is a value often passed to a function or subroutine in computer programming. In the example below, "3" is an argument passed to the function addNum.

```
def addNum(firstNum, secondNum):
    return firstNum + secondNum

print (addNum(3, 3))
```

Arithmetic Logic Unit See ALU.

Arithmetic Operator multiplication (*), division (/), addition (+), subtraction (-).

Arithmetic Shift in binary is a shift of the bits to the left or right preserving the sign bit (MSB).

Areal Density is the amount of data stored on a hard disk per square inch, and is equal to the tracks per inch multiplied by the bits per inch along each track.

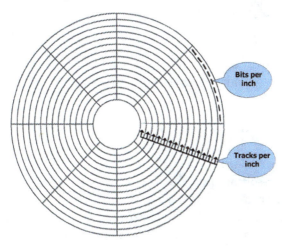

ARM is a family of high-performance RISC-based microprocessors often used in handheld devices such as PDAs tablets, some laptops and palmtops. .

ARP stands for Address resolution Protocol and is part of the TCP/IP suite used to map an IP address to the hardware MAC address.

Array is a data structure consisting of a collection of elements referenced by an index commonly used in computer programming to temporarily store data so it can be sorted or searched. Array [index]. This is a 1 dimensional array.

A 2 dimensional array has two indexes. Array [row] [col]

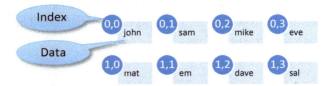

Artefact is caused by defects in compression or other digital processing. Common artefacts include jaggies, polygon shearing and pixelation.

Artificial Intelligence (AI). Refers to the simulation of human intelligence in machines, enabling them to perform tasks that typically require human intelligence, such as learning, reasoning, problem-solving, perception, understanding natural language, and decision-making. AI systems are designed to analyze large amounts of data, identify patterns, and make predictions or decisions based on that data without explicit programming. These systems often utilize techniques such as machine learning, neural networks, natural language processing, and robotics to mimic cognitive functions associated with human intelligence.

ASCII stands for American Standard Code for Information Interchange and is a data encoding standard developed by the American National Standards Institute (ANSI) describing how characters are represented on a computer. The original ASCII character set consists of 128 7-bit characters numbered from 0 to 127 which includes numerals, punctuation marks, upper and lowercase letters of the alphabet

Char	Code	Char	Code	Char	Code	Char	Code	Char	Code	Char	Code
0	48	C	67	O	79	a	97	m	109	y	121
1	49	D	68	P	80	b	98	n	110	z	122
2	50	E	69	Q	81	c	99	o	111	Space	32
3	51	F	70	R	82	d	100	p	112	!	33
4	52	G	71	S	83	e	101	q	113	"	34
5	53	H	72	T	84	f	102	r	114	#	35
6	54	I	73	U	85	g	103	s	115	$	36
7	55	J	74	V	86	h	104	t	116	%	37
8	56	K	75	W	87	i	105	u	117	&	38
9	57	L	76	X	88	j	106	v	118	'	39
A	65	M	77	Y	89	k	107	w	119	(	40
B	66	N	78	Z	90	l	108	x	120	)	41

The ASCII character set also includes special control codes such as a carriage return or a tab.

Char	Code	Char	Code	Char	Code
NUL (null)	0	FF (NP form feed new page)	12	CAN (cancel)	24
SOH (start of heading)	1	CR (carriage return)	13	EM (end of medium)	25
STX (start of text)	2	SO (shift out)	14	SUB (substitute)	26
ETX (end of text)	3	SI (shift in)	15	ESC (escape)	27
EOT (end of transmission)	4	DLE (data link escape)	16	FS (file separator)	28
ENQ (enquiry)	5	DC1 (device control 1)	17	GS (group separator)	29
ACK (acknowledge)	6	DC2 (device control 2)	18	RS (record separator)	30
BEL (bell)	7	DC3 (device control 3)	19	US (unit separator)	31
BS (backspace)	8	DC4 (device control 4)	20		
TAB (horizontal tab)	9	NAK (negative acknowledge)	21		
LF (NL line feed new line)	10	SYN (synchronous idle)	22		
VT (vertical tab)	11	ETB (end of trans. block)	23		

Aspect Ratio is the ratio of width of an image to the height. When an image is displayed on different size screens, the aspect ratio must be kept the same to avoid  stretching in either the vertical or horizontal direction. For most current monitors, this ratio 16:9.

Assembly Language is a low level programming language that uses mnemonics to represent instructions which are later assembled into machine code by and assembler. Each mnemonic such as LDA, represents a machine code instruction.

```
LDA 1000        // load ACC with value at address 1000
ADD 1001        // add value stored at address 1001
STO 1010        // store value in ACC at address 1010
END             // halt program
```

Assignment Operator is often used in computer programming to assign a value to a variable, the most common being an equals sign. There are also various other assignment operators.

Operator	Description	Example	Notes
=	Assigns values from the right side of equals sign (a+c) to the left (b)	b = a + c	assigns result of a + c to b
+=	Adds right operand (a) to the left operand (b) then assigns the result to left operand	b += a	same as b = b + a
-=	Subtracts right operand (a) from the left operand (b) then assigns the result to left operand	b -= a	same as b = b - a
*=	Multiplies right operand (a) with the left operand (b) then assigns the result to left operand	b *= a	same as b = b * a
/=	Divides left (b) operand with the right operand (a) then assigns the result to left operand	b /= a	same as b = b / a
%=	Takes modulus of the two operands then assigns the result to left operand	b %= a	same as b = b % a
**=	Performs an exponential calculation on operators then assigns value to the left operand	b **= a	same as b = b ** a
//=	Performs floor division on operators then assigns value to the left operand	b //= a	same as b = b // a

Astable an electronic device with two states used for timing in digital watches or a computer clock timing pulse. The 555 timer is an example of an astable integrated circuit.

Asymmetric Compression is a compression algorithm which requires more processing power and time to compress the data than to decompress it. It is often used to compress digital video and to backup files that are rarely decompressed.

Asymmetric Encryption also known as public-key encryption is a cryptographic encryption system that uses two keys: a private key and a public key, often used in SSL certificates for HTTPS.

This cryptographic system uses a pair of keys – a public key and a private key – to encrypt and decrypt data. The public key is used to encrypt data, while the private key is used to decrypt it. The public is freely distributed and shared with anyone, allowing others to encrypt messages or data. The data can only be decrypted using the corresponding private key.

Asynchronous refers to events that are not co-ordinated with a clock signal. Devices send and ACK to verify that a block of data has been sent.

Asynchronous Cache is SRAM that does not require a clock signal to validate its control signals. About 30% lower in price and performance compared to synchronous cache.

Asynchronous Communication is the transmission of data without the use of a clock signal, where data can be transmitted intermittently rather than in a steady stream.

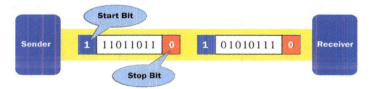

AT Bus started with the IBM-AT (Advanced Technology) systems. It is still the standard interface for most PC expansion cards. It is also known as the ISA (Industry Standard Architecture) bus.

AT Command Set was originally developed by Dennis Hayes and is the set of industry-standard commands used to control the modem. The command set consists of commands for dialing, hanging up, and changing the parameters of the connection. The vast majority of dial-up modems use the Hayes command set.

ATA stands for AT Attachment, the specification formulated in the 1980s by a consortium of hardware and software manufacturers, that defines the IDE drive interface. AT refers to the IBM PC/AT personal computer and its bus architecture. IDE drives are sometimes referred to as ATA drives or AT bus drives. The newer ATA-2 specification defines the EIDE interface, which improves upon the IDE standard. See also IDE and EIDE.

ATAPI stands for Advanced Technology Attachment Packet Interface, a specification that defines device side characteristics for an IDE connected peripheral, such as CD-ROM or tape drives. ATAPI is essentially an adaptation of the SCSI command set to the IDE interface.

Athlon XP is the line of 7th generation AMD processors, dating from the time of the Athlon CPU's transition from the Thunderbird core to the Palomino core in 2001.

ATM stands for Asynchronous Transfer Mode, a network switching technology used in telecommunication networks that transmit data in cells or packets of a fixed size over a virtual connection or circuit (VC). These connections are identified using a virtual path identifier (VPI) and a virtual channel identifier (VCI).

ATSC is an international, non-profit organisation responsible for developing voluntary standards for digital television in the USA, including the high definition television (HDTV) and standard definition television (SDTV) families of standards.

Attachment is a file such as a document or picture added to an email message.

ATX is short for **A**dvanced **T**echnology **E**xtended and is a specification used to outline motherboard and power supply configurations. ATX allows each manufacturer to put ports in a rectangular area on the back of the system. ATX power supplies produce three main outputs: 3.3v, 5v and 12v which are distributed to the motherboard using a 24 pin connector, an 8 pin auxiliary connector for the CPU and various connectors for disk drives and high end graphics cards. Shown below is a standard ATX or Full ATX board.

Audio Card also known as a sound card, is an internal expansion card that facilitates the input and output of audio signals to and from a computer, providing the audio for multimedia applications such as music, editing video or audio, presentations, games and video projection through a speaker or sound system. Audio devices are usually connected using 1/8" (3.5mm) audio jacks.

Audio Jack also known as a headphone jack or phone connector, is a family of electrical connectors typically used for analog audio signals. It is cylindrical in shape and comes in two standard sizes: 3.5mm (1/8 inch) and the larger 6.35mm (1/4 inch). Audio jacks can be designed to support various types of signals:

- TS (Tip-Sleeve): A two-conductor design that supports a single audio channel (mono).

- TRS (Tip-Ring-Sleeve): A three-conductor design that can carry two channels (stereo) or balanced audio signals.

- TRRS (Tip-Ring-Ring-Sleeve): A four-conductor design that provides additional functionality, such as a microphone input or video together with stereo audio.

Augmented Reality (AR). A technology that superimposes computer-generated images, sounds, or other sensory enhancements onto the real-world environment, typically viewed through digital devices such as smartphones, tablets, or specialized AR glasses.

Authentication Token is a unique piece of data issued by an authentication server and are used to prove the identity of the user and provide access to protected resources or functionalities within a system or application. They are typically included in HTTP headers or request parameters when accessing APIs or web services, allowing the server to verify the user's identity and authorize requested actions.

Authoring System a software application that allows developers to design interactive courseware easily without the need for computer programming skills.

Autoencoder is a type of artificial neural network used for unsupervised learning and dimensionality reduction tasks. It consists of an encoder network that compresses input data into a lower-dimensional representation, and a decoder network that reconstructs the original input from the compressed representation. Autoencoders are trained to minimize reconstruction error, forcing them to learn meaningful features and patterns in the input data.

Auto Refresh is a process used in Dynamic Random-Access Memory (DRAM) to maintain data integrity by periodically recharging the stored data in memory cells. Since DRAM stores data as electrical charges in capacitors, these charges naturally leak over time and require frequent refreshing to prevent data loss.

Autonomous Vehicles also known as self-driving cars or driverless vehicles, are vehicles equipped with sensors, cameras, GPS, and other technologies that enable them to navigate and operate without human intervention.

Automatic Speech Recognition (ASR) is a technology that enables computers to transcribe spoken language into text. ASR systems analyze audio signals, such as speech recordings or real-time audio streams, to identify spoken words and phrases and convert them into written text. ASR technology relies on machine learning algorithms, acoustic models, language models, and signal processing techniques to achieve accurate transcription results across different languages and dialects. ASR systems have diverse applications, including voice-activated assistants, dictation software, voice search, and captioning for multimedia content.

Autoscan is a microprocessor-based feature of some monitors incorporating automatic synchronisation of their horizontal and vertical frequencies with those of the installed video graphics adapter. An autoscan monitor can thus operate with a wide range of video adapters.

AV short for Audio Visual or Audio Video: refers to equipment used in audio and video applications, such as microphones, videotape machines (VCRs), sound systems and hard disk systems for storing digitised audio or video data.

Avatar. A graphical representation or digital persona that represents a user in a virtual environment, online community, or computer game. Avatars can be customized to reflect the user's appearance, identity, preferences, or personality traits, often through the selection of predefined features, attributes, or accessories. Avatars enable users to interact with others, navigate virtual spaces, and engage in activities or experiences without revealing their real-world identities. Avatars are commonly used in virtual reality (VR) environments, social media platforms, online forums, and multiplayer online games, enhancing immersion, social interaction, and personalization

AVC short for Advanced Video Coding also known as MPEG-4 AVC, MPEG-4 part 10 or H.264, and is a widely used standard for encoding of high resolution video used in digital video broadcast, streaming, and storage. See MPEG, H.264.

Average Seek Time is the average time it takes for the read/write head to move to a specific location. To compute the average seek time, divide the time it takes to complete a large number of random seeks by the number of seeks performed.

AVI short for Audio Video Interleaved and is Microsoft's file format for digital video and audio for Windows. AVI files contain blocks of video and audio data are interlaced together using less compression than H264 or MPEG.

AWG short for American Wire Gauge and is a standard measuring gauge for certain conductors such as copper. The higher the AWG number the thinner the wire. The origins of the gauge lie in the number of times the wire ran through a wire machine to reduce its diameter. Thus a 24-guage wire was thinner than an 18-guage wire because it ran through a wire machine 6 more times.

AWS (Amazon Web Services) is a cloud computing platform and suite of services offered by Amazon.com. AWS provides a wide range of infrastructure services, including computing power, storage, databases, networking, machine learning, and analytics, delivered over the internet on a pay-as-you-go basis. AWS enables organizations to build, deploy, and scale applications and services quickly and cost-effectively, without the need to invest in physical infrastructure or manage complex IT infrastructure. AWS services are used by millions of customers worldwide, ranging from startups to large enterprises, across various industries.

Azure is a cloud computing platform and services offered by Microsoft Corporation. Azure provides a comprehensive suite of cloud services, including computing, storage, databases, networking, AI, machine learning, Internet of Things (IoT), and developer tools, delivered over the internet on a subscription basis. Azure enables organizations to build, deploy, and manage applications and services across a global network of data centers, with scalability, reliability, and security built-in. Azure services support a wide range of programming languages, frameworks, and operating systems, making it a popular choice for cloud computing solutions.

B

B Channel is an ISDN communication channel that carries voice, circuit or packet conversations. The B-channel is the fundamental component of ISDN interfaces. It carries 64,000 bits per seconds in either direction.

Baby AT is the form factor used by most PC motherboards in the early 1990s. The original motherboard for the PC-AT measured 12in by 13in. Baby AT motherboards are a little smaller, 8.5in by 11in.

Back Buffer is a buffer used in double-buffering. Graphics are drawn into the back buffer so that the rendering process cannot be seen by the user. When the drawing is complete, the front and back buffers are swapped.

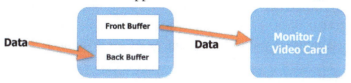

Backdoor is a means of access to a computer system that bypasses the installed security measures often exploited by a hacker or cyber criminal.

Backlight is the light source on an LCD screen. The backlight illuminates the screen from behind the LCD panel

Backside Bus is a dedicated channel between olcer CPUs and a Level 2 cache. The dual independent bus (DIB) architecture allows a processor to use both the backside bus and the frontside bus simultaneously.

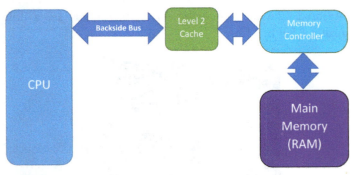

Backup is a copy of a file, directory, or volume on a separate storage device from the original, for the purpose of retrieval in case the original is accidentally erased, damaged, or destroyed. Backups can be made on tape drives, NAS drives, external hard drives to name a few. There are different types of backups. You could take a full backup which copies every single file on the system, or an incremental backup which only copies the changes since the last backup.

Backup Utility is a computer program used to create backups of data.

BACP short for Bandwidth Allocation Control Protocol and is a protocol that works in conjunction with Multilink PPP to manage bandwidth dynamically. BACP lets two devices negotiate the bandwidth as needed.

Bad Block is a block on a disk that cannot reliably hold data because of a flaw or damage.

Bad Track Table is a label affixed to the casing of a hard disk drive that tells which tracks are flawed and cannot hold data. The list is typed into the low-level formatting program when the drive is being installed.

Banding is a defect commonly found in inkjet printers that causes horizontal or vertical lines to appear on printouts usually caused by print head blockage or head misalignment.

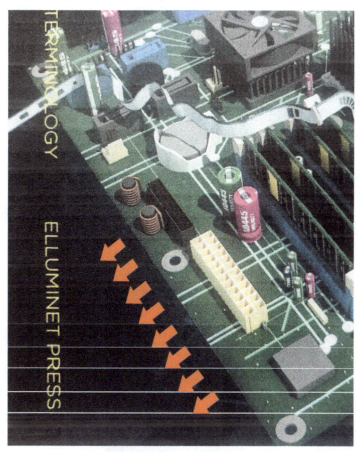

Bandwidth is the amount of data that can move through a particular interface in a given period of time, e.g. a 64-bit wide, 100 MHz SDRAM data bus has a bandwidth of 800 MBps.

Barcode is a machine readable code consisting of black vertical lines often to identify a product. The first two digits are assigned country codes or official standards agency in that country. 978 is an ISBN for a book, 0 is a US/Canadian product, 50 is UK. The rest makes up the manufacturer ID and item code. The last digit is an error check.

Barrel Distortion is an image distortion where the image is bowed outwards, towards the edges of the screen.

Baseband is a transmission system that only uses a single signal on the cable at a time. A common example is the Ethernet protocol, which transfers data using a baseband signal - 100BaseT.

Baud Rate is the number of symbols transmitted per second. This is not always the same as the bps rate (see also bps), because a given symbol, or baud, may have more than one bit.

BBS short for Bulletin Board System and was a site that allowed multiple users to connect to using a terminal program where they could download software, leave messages for other users, and exchange information. Bulletin Boards proliferated in the 1980s before the introduction of the world wide web. A BBS functions somewhat like a stand-alone web site with text, ASCII graphics and menu systems. Many BBSes also offered online games in which users can compete with each other.

BCC stands for Blind Carbon Copy and is used in email systems to allow the sender to send a copy of the email without the recipient knowing.

Bernoulli Drive named after a Swiss scientist who discovered the principle of aerodynamic lift. The principal characteristic of a Bernoulli drive is that the flexible disk floats between the read/write heads, so there is no actual contact, making it is less susceptible to head crashes. Bernoulli technology was used in Iomega's Bernoulli Box drives, which preceded Zip drives.

Bezel is a name for the border around the edge of the screen. Also used to describe the rim around the edge of faceplates, and drive bays.

Bezier is a curve named after Pierre Bézier, who used the technique the 1960s for designing curves for the bodywork of Renault cars. Today bezier curves are used in graphics programs such as Adobe Illustrator.

BGA short for Ball Grid Array and is a specification for pin layouts on micro chips, such as those used on a CPU chip.

Bifringence is the property of a material which causes incident light waves of different polarisations to be refracted differently by the material.

Big Data refers to large and complex datasets that cannot be processed or analyzed using traditional data processing techniques. These datasets are characterized by their volume, velocity, variety, and veracity. Big Data analytics involves the use of advanced tools and technologies to extract insights, patterns, and trends from massive datasets for decision-making, forecasting, and optimization. Big Data applications span various industries, including finance, healthcare, marketing, and research, and rely on technologies such as distributed computing, machine learning, and data mining for processing and analysis.

Bi-linear Filtering improves the look of blocky, low-resolution 3D textures when viewed close up by blending and interpolating groups of texels to create a smoother image.

Binary refers to a number system that consists of only two digits: 0 and 1. This base-2 numeral system forms the basis of all binary code, which is used to represent data in virtually all computer systems and digital devices. Each digit in a binary number is known as a bit, the smallest unit of data in computing, which can either represent a state of off (0) or on (1). In computing contexts, binary numbers are often used to operate, manipulate, and store data, serving as the fundamental language through which computers communicate and process information.

Binary Addition. Adding two binary numbers together is fairly straight forward. All you have to remember are these simple rules...

0 + 0 = 0
0 + 1 = 1
1 + 0 = 1
1 + 1 = 0 carry 1
1 + 1 + 1 = 1 carry 1

Have a look at adding these two numbers together, and apply the rules quoted above.

Working from the right to the left we get:

0+1=1, 0+1=1, 1+1=0 carry 1, 1+1+0=0 carry 1

Once you work through the steps, you'll end up with something like this:

Binary Coded Decimal (BCD) is a class of binary encodings of decimal numbers where each decimal digit is represented by a fixed number of binary digits, usually four or eight. In BCD, each digit of a decimal number is represented by its own binary sequence, making it straightforward to convert between decimal and binary systems, especially for digital displays. BCD is used in systems where a precise decimal representation is required, and arithmetic operations are performed on digits separately, such as in calculators and digital clocks.

For example:

21_{10} would be 0010 0001

The "2" is encoded as 0010_2 and the "1" is encoded as 0001_2

Binary Multiplication Multiplying binary numbers together is fairly straight forward. All you have to remember are these simple rules...

0 x 0 = 0
0 x 1 = 0
1 x 0 = 0
1 x 1 = 1

Lets try an example. Multiply 101 x 11
First we multiply 101 by the first 1, following the rules above.

101
  11 x
 101

Then on the next line, we put a 0 as a place-holder

 101
  11 x
 101
   0 <-- add place-holder

Then multiply 101 by second 1, which produces 101.

101
 11 x
 101
1010 +

Once you've done the that, add the two together (101 + 1010)

 101
 11 x
 101
1010 +
1111

So 101 x 11 = 1111   (in decimal 5 x 3 = 15)

Binary Search is an efficient algorithm used for finding an item in a sorted list. It works by repeatedly dividing the list in half. If the value being searched for is less than the middle value in the list, the search continues on the left half; otherwise, it continues on the right half. During each step, the algorithm compares the value being searched for to the middle element of the list. For example:

If we search for 14. Find middle of array, check to see if 14 is greater or less than 22.

1	2	4	12	14	**22**	24	56	66	88	90

14<22

In this case it is less, so discard right hand side of array

1	2	**4**	12	14

14>4

Repeat process, this time it's greater so discard left hand side. Keep repeating until you end up with the searched value.

12	14

14>12

14

47

Binary Shift is a way of multiplying or dividing binary numbers. To multiply a number by 2, shift all the digits in the binary number along to the left and fill the gaps after the shift with a 0. This is also known as a logical shift and is best used on unsigned binary numbers. To multiply by 4 shift the digits two places.

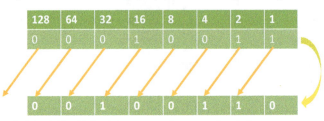

To divide shift all the binary numbers to the right.

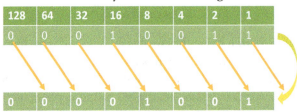

Binary Tree is a tree data structure in which each leaf or node has at most two children, commonly used in sorting and compression algorithms such as a binary search tree or in huffman coding.

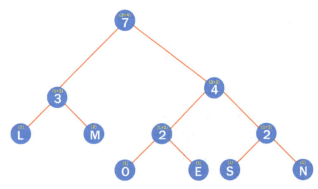

Biometric is a device often used in user authentication and works by scanning a finger print, face, or retina.

BIOS a small program stored in permanent ROM and is soldered directly onto the motherboard. BIOS Stands for Basic Input Output System and is responsible for checking hardware components at bootup, called a power on self test (POST).

BIOS flashing is the process of upgrading the firmware of a computer's BIOS (Basic Input/Output System) to install new features, improve compatibility, or fix security vulnerabilities. It involves overwriting the existing BIOS firmware with a newer version provided by the motherboard manufacturer or a third-party vendor. BIOS flashing can be performed using specialized software tools provided by the manufacturer, typically from within the BIOS setup utility or through a bootable USB drive. However, BIOS flashing carries risks, as improper flashing or interruption during the process can result in system instability or even permanent damage to the motherboard. Therefore, it is essential to follow proper procedures and precautions when performing BIOS flashing.

BISYNC short for BInary SYNChronous: a major category of synchronous communications protocols, developed by IBM and used in mainframe networks. Bisync communications require that both sending and receiving devices are synchronised before transmission of data is started. Contrast with asynchronous transmission.

Bit is short for binary digit, and is basic unit of data storage. A bit can either be a 1 or 0. There are 8 bits in 1 byte.

Bit Depth in colour images, is the number of colours used to represent the image. Typical values are 8-, 16- and 24-bit colour, allowing 256, 65,536 and 16,777,216 colours to be represented. The latter is known as true colour, because 16.8 million different colours is about as many as the human eye can distinguish. Devices that support 32-bit colour use an 8-bit alpha channel to define a possible 256 levels of opacity. Also referred to as colour depth.

Bit/s stands for Bits Per Second and is the speed at which data travels over a communications line. For example, a modem that operates at 9600 bits per second can transfer 9600 binary digits each second. A character normally consists of eight bits, plus the start and stop bits that separate the character from other transmitted characters.

Bitmap also known as a raster image, uses thousands of pixels in varying colours and intensities to represent an image. Each pixel on screen is represented by a number of bits. Each pixel can be represented by one bit (simple black and white) or up to 32 bits (high-definition colour). A raw image bitmap commonly uses the file extension "bmp". Many image file formats use compressed bitmap variants, often with additional meta-data such as GIF, JPEG, EXIF, PNG, and TIFF.

Bleeding is a print distortion where adjacent colours run or merge into one another usually caused by excess ink or paper which is too absorbent.

Blockchain is a decentralized and distributed digital ledger technology that records transactions across multiple computers in a way that ensures security, transparency, and immutability. Each block in the chain contains a cryptographic hash of the previous block, a timestamp, and transaction data. Once recorded, the data in any given block cannot be altered without altering all subsequent blocks, which requires the consensus of the network majority. Blockchain technology is the foundation of cryptocurrencies like Bitcoin and has applications beyond digital currencies, including supply chain management, voting systems, and smart contracts.

Block Data is organised into logical "blocks" for transmission between devices. Blocks may be fixed or variable length, with block sizes of 512 or 1024 bytes being particularly common. An example of a block format is: preamble, user data, CRC, postamble.

Blockiness is the consequence of portions of an image breaking into little squares due to over-compression or a video file overwhelming a computer's processor. See also Artefact.

Blooming is a problem where bright white areas have a slight halo around them.

BLT stands for Bit-aLigned Block Transfer and is the process of copying pixels or other data from one place in memory to another.

Blue Screen of Death (BSoD) is a critical system error message displayed on Microsoft Windows operating systems when the system encounters a fatal error from which it cannot recover safely. When a BSoD occurs, the computer halts all operations, displays a blue screen with diagnostic information, and prompts the user to restart the system. The BSoD typically includes error codes, hexadecimal memory addresses, and information about the cause of the crash, such as faulty hardware, device driver issues, or software conflicts. BSoD errors can result from various factors, including hardware failures, incompatible software, corrupted system files, or system overheating. Resolving BSoD issues often requires troubleshooting techniques, such as system restore, or reinstalling the operating system.

Bluetooth is a wireless technology for exchanging data over short distances using a frequency of 2.4 to 2.485 GHz. This is often referred to as a PAN (or personal area network) and can be used to connect headphones, wireless mice, smart phones and make small data transfers.

Bluray is an optical storage medium used to store digital data such as computer files, software, videos and high definition films (720p and 1080p). They look very similar to DVDs except they have a greater storage capacity. Single-layer blurays can store up to 25GB. Dual layer discs can store up to 50GB.

BNC is a connector used for composite video on commercial video devices.

Was also used as a video connection type consisting of five separate cables for red, green, blue, and horizontal/vertical synchronisation signals on high end monitors.

BNF stands for Backus–Naur form and is often used to describe the syntax of programming languages, communication protocols, instruction sets and document formats. For example:

`<postal-address> ::= <name> <street> <code>`

Meaning a postal address consists of a name, followed by a street name, then a zip/post code.

Boolean Logic Named after the nineteenth-century mathematician George Boole, Boolean logic is a branch of algebra used for evaluating true/false statements using the operators AND, OR, NOT, NAND, NOR, XOR.. Boolean Logic is often used to evaluate logic gates when building electronic circuits.

Boot Drive The drive that the operating system first loads from (usually labelled "C" on a Windows machine).

Boot Sector is a reserved sector on a disk that is used to load the operating system. On start-up, the computer looks for the master book record (MBR) which is typically the first sector in the first partition of the disk. The MBR points to the first sector of the partition that contains the operating system (derived from the phrase "pulling yourself up from your bootstraps").

Bootloader is the program responsible for loading the operating system.

Bootstrapping, in the context of computing, refers to the process by which a computer system initializes itself and loads the operating system into memory. During the bootstrapping process, the computer's hardware components are initialized, memory is configured, and the system BIOS or firmware performs a power-on self-test (POST) to check for hardware integrity. Subsequently, the bootloader, a small program stored in non-volatile memory, is executed to locate and load the operating system kernel into memory, initiating the operating system's startup sequence.

Bot or internet bot is a program that runs automated tasks on the internet.

Botnet is a network of computers or devices that have been infected with malicious software (malware) and controlled remotely by a single entity, typically a cybercriminal or hacker. Botnets are often used to carry out coordinated attacks, such as distributed denial-of-service (DDoS) attacks, spam campaigns, or data theft. Infected devices, known as "bots" or "zombies," can be used to propagate the malware, steal sensitive information, or execute malicious commands without the knowledge of their owners. Botnets pose significant cybersecurity threats and require proactive measures for detection, mitigation, and prevention.

BPI stands for Bits Per Inch and is a measure of how densely information is packed on a storage medium. See also Flux Density.

BPP stands for Bits Per Pixel and is the number of bits used to represent the colour value of each pixel in a digitised image.

bps is short for Bits Per Second and is the speed at which data is transferred to and from a storage medium or over a network. Note lowercase "b" indicates bits.

Bps is short for Bytes per second. Capital "B" indicates bytes. The speed at which data is transferred to and from a storage medium or over a network.

Breakpoint. In software development and debugging, a breakpoint is a designated point or line in the source code where program execution can be paused or halted for inspection, analysis, or debugging purposes. Breakpoints are set by developers or debuggers using integrated development environments (IDEs) or debugging tools to identify and troubleshoot errors, bugs, or unexpected behavior in the program. When a breakpoint is encountered during program execution, the debugger suspends execution, allowing developers to examine variable values, step through code, evaluate expressions, and diagnose issues interactively. Breakpoints facilitate efficient debugging and software quality assurance during the development process.

BRI stands for Basic-Rate Interface and is the basic ISDN setup, consisting of two 64 Kbit/s B-channels (bearer channels), which carry data and voice in both directions, and one 16 Kbit/s D-channel, which carries call- control information. See also PRI.

Bridge is a device that operates at the data link layer (Layer 2) of the OSI 7 layer model and whose function is to connect and pass packets of information between two networks.

Brightness is a measure of the overall intensity of an image. The lower the brightness value, the darker the image. The higher the value, the lighter the image.

Broadband often refers to a high-speed internet connection that has a significantly greater bandwidth capacity for data transmission compared to traditional dial-up connections. It enables fast and efficient internet access, allowing users to download and upload large amounts of data, stream high-definition multimedia content, participate in video conferencing, and engage in online gaming with minimal latency. Broadband connections typically utilize technologies such as Digital Subscriber Line (DSL), cable modem, fiber optic, satellite, or wireless broadband to deliver high-speed internet access to users. Broadband connections offer faster download and upload speeds, greater reliability, and the ability to support multiple devices simultaneously, making them essential for modern digital communication, entertainment, and productivity needs.

The term is also used to describe any communications channel that transmits multiple data signals at the same time. Contrast with Baseband.

Brotli: A lossless data compression algorithm developed by Google, primarily designed to achieve higher compression ratios than other compression algorithms such as gzip and deflate. It is particularly effective for compressing text-based content on the web, including HTML, CSS, JavaScript, and font files. It utilizes a combination of modern compression techniques, including a context modeling approach based on the Lempel-Ziv (LZ77) algorithm, static dictionary, and Huffman coding, to achieve superior compression performance. Brotli compression results in smaller file sizes, reducing bandwidth usage, improving website loading times, and enhancing overall web performance. It is supported by major web browsers, web servers, and content delivery networks (CDNs), making it a widely adopted standard for web content compression.

Bubble Jet is Canon's trade name for its thermal drop on demand inkjet printer technology. The ink is heated, which produces a bubble that expands and ejects the ink out of the nozzle. As the bubble cools, the vacuum created draws fresh ink back into the nozzle.

Bubble Sort is a simple sorting algorithm that repeatedly steps through the list, compares adjacent elements, and swaps them if they are in the wrong order. This is repeated until the list is sorted. The algorithm gets its name from the way smaller elements "bubble" to the top of the list with each pass.

For example if we consider this list: 21, 6, 2, 15

If we want to bubble sort this list into ascending order, we start by comparing the first number with the second number.

21

6   Compare. If first number > second number, swap

2

If the first number is greater than the second number, we swap the numbers.

```
6
21    Swap
2
```

Repeat the process with the second, third, and forth element, until you get to the end of the list. Then we go through the list again and repeat the process. You'll need to go through the list as many times as it takes until they're all in order.

So once complete, you'll end up with:

```
2, 6, 15, 21
```

This type of sort is inefficient.

Buffer sometimes known as a cache is a location used for temporary storing data that is read from or waiting to be written to another device. A buffer is used to speed up access to many devices such as a hard disk.

Buffer overflow is a type of software vulnerability that occurs when a program writes data beyond the boundaries of an allocated buffer in memory. This can lead to corruption of adjacent memory locations, crashes, or even execution of arbitrary code by attackers.

Bug is an error in a computer program that causes erratic in correct results or a crash.

Bump Mapping in computer graphics is a 3D lighting technique designed to give a texture a three-dimensional, animated feel.

Burn is the process of writing data to a writable optical disk such as a DVD-R or CD-R

Burst Mode a rapid data-transfer technique that automatically generates a block of data (a series of consecutive addresses) every time the processor requests a single address. The assumption is that the next data-address the processor will request will be sequential to the previous one. Burst mode can be applied to both read operations (from memory) and write operations (to memory).

Bus refers to a communication pathway or interface that allows data to be transferred between various components of a computer system, such as the CPU, memory, and peripherals. The connection is made up of a set of wires called lines that can only carry 1 bit at a time. So a bus can have 32 or 64 different lines, hence we get 32 bit buses and 64 bit buses. There are many different kinds of bus including data bus, address bus, control bus, ISA, EISA, MCA, and the PCI-Express bus.

Bus Master IDE is the capability of a drive to effect data transfers from disk to memory with minimum intervention by the CPU known as Direct Memory Access (DMA) transfers.

Bus Topology is a network configuration in which all the devices are connected to a single cable called a bus

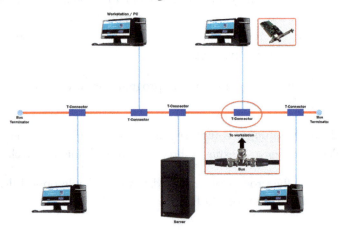

Byte is fundamental unit of digital information storage in computing. It consists of 8 bits, each of which can represent a binary value of either 0 or 1.

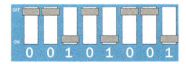

Bytes are used to encode characters, numbers, and other data in computer systems. They serve as the basic building blocks for representing and processing information in binary form. In most computer architectures, bytes are grouped together to form larger units of storage, such as kilobytes (KB), megabytes (MB), gigabytes (GB), and so on, which are used to quantify data storage capacities. Bytes play a crucial role in various computing operations, including data processing, memory storage, and communication between devices.

Bytecode is a binary representation of a program that is intermediate between source code and machine code. It is generated by compilers and used by virtual machines (VMs) to execute programs written in high-level programming languages. Bytecode allows for platform-independent execution of programs, as it can be interpreted or compiled to machine code by the VM on different operating systems or hardware architectures. Examples of languages that use bytecode include Java (compiled to Java bytecode) and Python (compiled to Python bytecode).

Bzip2 is a lossless data compression algorithm and software tool used for compressing and decompressing files. It is based on the Burrows-Wheeler transform and Huffman coding techniques, offering higher compression ratios compared to traditional compression methods like gzip. Bzip2 is commonly used to compress large files or archives for storage or transmission over the internet. It is often found in Unix-like operating systems and is supported by various file archiving utilities.

C

C is a general-purpose, procedural computer programming language developed at Bell Labs by Dennis Ritchie.

C++ is a general-purpose high level object oriented programming language created by Bjarne Stroustrup as an extension of the C programming language.

Cable Modem is a device that delivers high-speed Internet to your home using coaxial cables, often the same cables used to deliver cable TV.

Cache is an intermediate storage capacity between the processor and the RAM or disk drive. The most commonly used instructions are held here, allowing for faster processing.

Cache Buffer is intermediate storage between the processor and the disk drive used to store data likely to be requested next. Also known as Data Buffer. See also Look Ahead.

Cache Controller is the circuit that controls the interface between the CPU, cache and main memory (RAM) .

Cache Hit is when the address requested by the CPU is found in cache. Conversely, cache miss is when it's not found.

Cache Memory is a small block of high-speed memory (usually SRAM) located between the CPU and main memory that is used to store frequently requested data and instructions. Properly designed, a cache improves system performance by reducing the need to access the system's slower main memory for every transaction.

Camera an optical device used to capture an image. In 3D graphics, the viewpoint through which a scene is viewed. Flythroughs of scenes are conceptually a moving camera.

Candela is a unit of measurement of the intensity of light. An ordinary wax candle generates one candela. The maximum brightness for CRTs is about 100 to 120 cd/m2 and for TFTs, up to 250 cd/m2.

CAP short for Carrierless Amplitude Phase and is a multilevel multiphase encoding method used with ADSL technology. CAP uses amplitude and phase modulation techniques for sending signals over standard copper twisted-copper wire, giving data bit combinations a form of both amplitude and phase. Unlike DMT, CAP uses the whole frequency range from 4KHz up to 1.1MHz as a single channel. It is used in the V.32/V.32bis modem communication standard.

Capacitor is an electronic component that holds a charge.

Capacity is the amount of data that can be stored on a storage device. Capacity is usually expressed in megabytes, gigabytes or terabytes depending on the size.

Captcha is a test that includes an image of distorted text used to determine whether a user is human or an automated bot. These captcha tests are usually included in online forms or account sign in pages. The user must decipher the text and enter it into the field.

Carrier is the base signal used to transmit data across a telephone line. The modem modulates this signal (alters its frequency or phase) to encode the data to be transmitted.

CAS short for Column Address Select (or Strobe) and is a control pin on a DRAM memory module used to latch and activate a column address. The column selected on a DRAM module is determined by the data present at the address pins when CAS becomes active. Used with RAS and a row-address to select a bit within the DRAM.

CAT5 cables, introduced in the 1990s, are 4-pair twisted cables capable of supporting speeds up to 1000 Mbps with a frequency of up to 100 MHz. Primarily used in early Fast Ethernet implementations, CAT5 was a significant improvement over its predecessors, offering more reliable data transmission over longer distances. Despite its advances, CAT5 has largely been replaced by CAT5e due to its limitations in handling higher data rates required by modern network. The cables are terminated with a standard RJ45 connector.

CAT5e, an enhanced version of the CAT5 cable, supports networking speeds of up to 1 Gbps (1000 Mbps) and a frequency of up to 100 MHz. Introduced to reduce crosstalk (interference between the wires within the cable), CAT5e provides improved performance for 1000Base-T (Gigabit Ethernet) networks. Its backward compatibility with CAT5 infrastructure and cost-effectiveness have made CAT5e a widespread choice for residential and commercial networking needs, including internet connections, VoIP, and video surveillance systems.

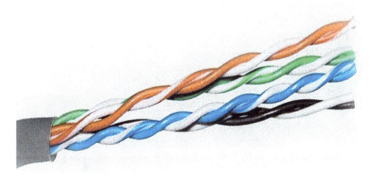

CAT6

CAT6 cables were designed to support higher data transmission speeds of up to 1 Gbps for lengths up to 100 meters and can achieve speeds of up to 10 Gbps in shorter runs (up to 55 meters). Operating at a frequency of up to 250 MHz, CAT6 includes improvements such as better insulation and thinner wires, which help in reducing crosstalk and allowing for better overall network performance. CAT6 is suitable for applications requiring high data rates, such as office buildings and data centers, where it supports advanced networking technologies including Gigabit Ethernet and beyond.

CAT6a extends the capabilities of CAT6 cables by doubling the frequency to 500 MHz and supporting data transmission speeds of up to 10 Gbps over 100 meters of cable length. This augmentation makes CAT6a an ideal choice for demanding network environments that require maximum speed and bandwidth, such as data centers and enterprise networks. The improved specifications of CAT6a help in reducing alien crosstalk, a type of interference from adjacent cables, and enable more reliable connections for high-speed networking applications.

CAT7 cables offer a significant leap in performance, supporting speeds of up to 10 Gbps over 100 meters of cable and a frequency of up to 600 MHz. CAT7 is designed with fully shielded twisted pairs (S/FTP), which provides a high level of protection against electromagnetic interference (EMI), making it suitable for environments with high EMI.  The shielding also minimizes crosstalk, ensuring high-speed data transmission is maintained. CAT7 is often used in data centers and server rooms where high-speed data transmission is critical.

CAT8 is the latest and most advanced category of Ethernet cable as of my last update, designed specifically for data center and high-performance networking applications. It supports bandwidths of up to 2 GHz (2000 MHz) and speeds of up to 25 Gbps or 40 Gbps over short distances of up to 30 meters. CAT8 cables are fully shielded with S/FTP construction, which drastically reduces alien crosstalk and improves signal integrity. This makes CAT8 an excellent choice for connecting switches, servers, and other high-speed networking equipment in data centers, offering the highest level of performance available.

Cathode in a CRT monitor and electrolytic cells, the cathode is negative. In a galvanic battery cell, the cathode is positive.

CCIA stands for Computer and Communications Industry Association and is a trade association composed of computer and communications firms. It represents their interests in domestic and foreign trade, and keeps members advised of relevant standards and regulatory policy.

CCIR is short for Comité Consultatif International pour la Radio.

CCIR 601 is a recommendation developed by the International Radio Consultative Committee for the digitisation of colour video signals. The CCIR 601 recommendation deals with colour space conversion from RGB to VCrCb, the digital filters used for limiting the bandwidth, the sample rate (defined as 13.5 MHz), and the horizontal resolution (720 active pixels).

CCITT short for Consultative Committee for International Telephone and Telegraph and is an international standards organisation dedicated to creating communications protocols that will enable global compatibility for the transmission of voice, data, and video across all computing and telecommunications equipment. Changed its name to the International Telecommunications Union (ITU) in 1993.

CDMA stands for Code Division with Multiple Access and is a technology for digital transmission of radio signals that uses digital encoding and spread spectrum RF techniques to allow multiple users to share the same RF channel. In CDMA, a frequency is divided using codes, rather than time or frequency.

CDPD Cellular Digital Packet Data: a wireless communications protocol – widely used by law enforcement agencies – which enables users to transmit packets of data over the cellular network using a portable computing device and a CDPD modem.

CDTV Commodore Dynamic Total Vision: consumer multimedia system from Commodore that includes CD-ROM/ CD audio player, Motorola 68000 processor, 1MB RAM, and 10-key infrared remote control.

CeBIT A computer exhibition hosted in Hannover, Germany in the spring of each year. The exhibition is a spin-off from the more broadly-based Hannover Fair trade show and debuted in 1986.

Cellular Network or mobile network is a wireless network distributed over land which is divided into areas called cells.

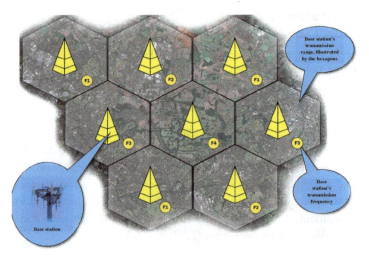

This is how a cell phone or mobile phone network operates. Each of these cells is assigned a frequency (eg F1-F4) each served by a radio base station. The frequencies can be reused in other cells, provided that the same frequencies are not reused in neighbouring cells as it would cause interference.

CELP (Code-Excited Linear Prediction) is a speech coding algorithm used to compress speech by modeling and encoding audio signals at low bitrates.

CentOS short for Community Enterprise Operating System, and is a Linux distribution based on the source code of Red Hat Enterprise Linux (RHEL). It is a free and open-source operating system known for its stability, reliability, and long-term support. CentOS aims to provide a platform suitable for both enterprise and community users, offering a robust and secure environment for various computing needs, including server deployments, desktop systems, and development environments.

Centralized Database refers to a data storage system where all data is stored and managed in a single location or repository. In this model, all data operations, including storage, retrieval, and management, are performed through a central server or database instance. Centralized databases offer several advantages, including simplified data management, consistent data access, and easier implementation of security measures and backup strategies. However, they also pose challenges such as potential single points of failure, scalability limitations, and increased network traffic.

Centronics Interface also known as a parallel port is a 36-pin connection designed by Centronics Corporation and was used to connect a printer to a computer. Somewhat obsolete nowadays.

CGA is a low-resolution video display standard, invented for the first IBM PC. CGA's highest resolution mode is 2 colours at a resolution of 640 x 200 pixels.

CGI (graphics) Short for Computer Generated Imagery. The use of 3D modelling to create characters, objects and environments for use in films and television programs, videos, or computer games.

CGI (web) Common Gateway Interface: a standard method of extending Web server functionality by executing programs or scripts on a Web server in response to Web browser requests. A common use of CGI is in form processing, where the browser sends the form data to a CGI script on the server, and the script integrates the data with a database and sends back a results page as HTML.

CGM short for Computer Graphics Metafile and is a standard format that allows for graphics images.

CGMS short for Copy Guard Management System and is a method of preventing copies or controlling the number of sequential copies allowed.

CGMS/A is added to an analogue signal (such as line 21 of NTSC).

CGMS/D is added to a digital signal, such as IEEE 1394.

Chapter is a subdivisions of a video title (e.g. movie) on a DVD-Video disc, each chapter being a scene or other section as defined during authoring.

Character is a unit of information such as a letter of the alphabet, numeric digit, or punctuation symbol.

Character Recognition is the process of scanning typed or handwritten text into machine encoded characters

Character Set is a complete list of characters that are recognised by a computer such as ASCII or Unicode.

Check bit or parity bit is an extra data bit added to a string or binary code used to check for errors in an electronic transmission or data storage.

Chipset is the electronic component mounted on a motherboard that manages the flow of data between the processor, memory and other peripherals.

Chorus is a doubling effect used to enhance sound.

Chroma is the colour portion of a video signal that includes hue and saturation information. Requires luminance, or light intensity, to make it visible. Also referred to as Chrominance.

Chrome Google Chrome is a freely available web browser developed by Google and is available for Windows, Mac, Linux, iOS, Android and Chromebook.

ChromeBook is a tablet or laptop style computer running the ChromeOS operating system.

ChromeOS is a linux based operating system developed by Google for the Chromebook. ChromeOS supports both android apps from the google play store, and linux apps.

CIDR Stands for Classless Inter-Domain Routing and is an alternative IP addressing scheme that allows a more efficient allocation of IP addresses than the class based method.

CIDR notation	Netmask notation	Available hosts	Notes
/0	0.0.0.0	4,294,967,294	Max hosts with IPv4
/8	255.0.0.0	16,777,214	Class A
/16	255.255.0.0	65,533	Class B
/24	255.255.255.0	254	Class C
/25	255.255.255.128	126	
/26	255.255.255.192	62	
/27	255.255.255.224	30	
/28	255.255.255.240	14	
/29	255.255.255.248	6	
/30	255.255.255.252	2	

For example, the class C IP address 192.168.1.1 could be associated with the subnet mask of 255.255.255.0.

Meaning 192.168.1 represent the network, and the last digit represents the host. You'd express this as 192.168.1.1/24 using the CIDR notation. It means the first 24 bits of the IP address represent the network.

CIE stands for Commission International de l'Eclairage: the international organisation that establishes methods for measuring colour. Their colour standards for colourmetric measurements are internationally accepted specifications that define colour values mathematically.

CIELAB (L*a*b*) is a colour model to approximate human vision. The model consists of three variables: L* for luminosity, a* for one colour axis, and b* for the other colour axis. CIELAB is a good model of the Munsell colour system and human vision.

CIELUV (L*u*v) is a colour space model produced in 1978 by the CIE at the same time as the L*a*b model. CIE L*u*v is used with colour monitors, whereas CIE L*a*b is used with colour print production.

CIF stands for Common Interchange Format and is a standard format for picture resolution, frame rate, and the colour space of digital video.

Circuit Switching is a transmission method used to send a message over a dedicated physical path between the sender and receiver. Contrast with packet switching.

CISC stands for Complex Instruction Set Computer. This architecture uses complex instructions, meaning a single instruction can execute several operations such as a load data from memory, perform an operation, and store result in memory.

```
ADD 1000, 1001
```

Most modern computers such as PCs, Macs, and Laptops use the CISC architecture.

Clean Room An environmentally controlled dust-free assembly or repair facility in which hard disk drives are assembled or can be opened for internal servicing.

Clear To Send CTS is an RS-232C signal that tells the computer it can start sending information. See also Request To Send (RTS).

CLI stands for Command Line Interface and is a text-based interface where the user types in various commands to execute tasks or run programs. Examples include MS-DOS Command Prompt, Windows PowerShell, MacOS Terminal, and Linux Terminal.

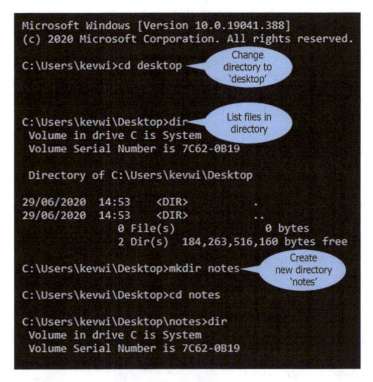

Client is any computer, device or program that uses the services of another program, computer or server..

Client-Server is a network architecture in which each computer or process on the network is either a "client" or a "server". Servers are powerful computers or processes dedicated to managing disk drives (file servers), printers (print servers), or network traffic (network servers). Clients are typically PCs or workstations on which users run applications. Contrast Peer-to-peer.

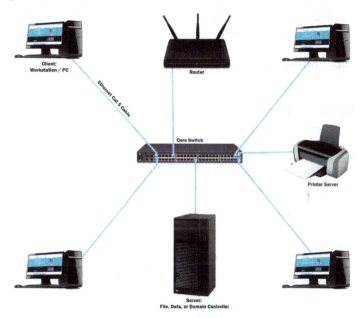

Clip Art is a library of icons, buttons, and other pre-made images that can be inserted into documents.

Clipping in audio production is the distortion that occurs when an audio signal is boosted beyond its capacity.

 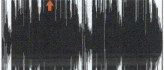

Clock is a microchip or crystal that generates a regular pulse to coordinate the functions and timing in a computer system.

Clock Doubling boosts CPU performance by increasing the internal CPU clock, while maintaining the same I/O speed (for compatibility).

Clock Rate is the number of pulses emitted from a computer's clock in one second; it determines the rate at which logical or arithmetic gating is performed in a synchronous computer.

Clock Speed is the speed at which the CPU executes instructions, usually measured in GHz.

Clone is any computer system compatible with the IBM PC standard.

Cloud is a service where data is stored remotely on servers managed and maintained by a cloud storage provider such as Dropbox, OneDrive or GoogleDrive. You connect to these services from your computer and save files to the cloud service rather than to your local machine.

Cluster is a group of sectors on a hard disk drive that is addressed as one logical unit by the operating system.

CMD or the Command Key is a modifier key on a Mac used in some keyboard shortcuts. Equivalent to the CTRL key on a PC.

CMOS stands for Complementary Metal Oxide Semiconductor: a process that uses both N- and P-channel devices in a complimentary fashion to achieve small geometries and low power consumption. CMOS is commonly used on PC motherboards and is a battery powered chip that stores the BIOS settings and hardware configuration information as well as the current time and date. The chip itself is either a separate microchip mounted on the motherboard or build into the south bridge. A CR 2032 3V coin shaped battery is often mounted on a computer's motherboard to power the CMOS RAM.

CMOS RAM is Complementary Metal Oxide Semiconductor Random Access Memory: a bank of memory that stores a PC's BIOS configuration information, including type identifiers for the drives installed in the PC, and the amount of RAM present. It also maintains the correct date, time and hard drive information for the system.

CMY is a cheaper, single cartridge inkjet that uses the Cyan Magenta Yellow model. Black here is referred to as composite black and is made up from the three colours. Dye-sublimation uses these three colours on the print ribbon.

CMYK Cyan, Magenta, Yellow, Black: the four process colours that are used in four-colour printed reproduction. By overlaying or dithering combinations of these four inks in different proportions, a vast range of colours can be created.

CNAME Record Short for Canonical Name, is a record on a DNS server used to create an alias and is commonly used to map a subdomain to a domain. Eg to map elluminetpress.com to www.elluminetpress.com, or create a subdomain such as mail.elluminetpress.com or store.elluminetpress.com

Records

Type	Name	Value	TTL	
A	elluminetpress.com	63.63.202.63	1 Hour	✎
CNAME	www	elluminetpress.com	1 Hour	✎

CO stands for Central Office, a facility that serves local telephone subscribers. In the CO, subscribers' lines are joined to switching equipment that allows them to connect to each other for both local and long distance calls.

COAST stands for Cache On A Stick and was a popular design specification for plug in L2 cache modules.

Coaxial Cable is cable consisting of a hollow outer cylindrical conductor that surrounds a single inner wire conductor. Two types of coaxial cable are currently used in LANs: 50-ohm cable, which is used for digital signalling, and 75-ohm cable, which is used for analogue signalling and high-speed digital signalling.

Codec is short for COmpression-DECompression, and is an algorithm used to compresses and decompresses video or audio data to conserve bandwidth on a transmission medium such as the internet, and for storage on a disk drive. H264, QuickTime and Video for Windows are examples.

Collision is a situation that occurs when two or more devices attempt to send a signal along the same channel at the same time. The result of a collision is generally a garbled message. All computer networks require some sort of mechanism to either prevent collisions altogether or to recover from collisions when they do occur.

Colour Balance is the process of matching the amplitudes of red, green and blue signals so the resulting mixture makes an accurate white colour.

Colour Cycling is a means of simulating motion in a video by changing colours.

Colour Keying is to superimpose one image over another for special effects. For example in movie production, subjects are usually shot against a blue or green screen allowing the editor to remove the blue/green colour and replace it with a computer generated background or scene.

Colour Palette also called a colour lookup table (CLUT), index map, or colour map, it is a commonly-used method for saving file space when creating colour images. Instead of each pixel containing its own RGB values, which would require 24 bits, each pixel holds an 8- bit value, which is an index number into the colour palette. The colour palette contains a 256-colour subset of the 16 million unique displayable colours.

Colour Temperature defines the whiteness of the white on the screen. Variations are measured in degrees Kelvin. Natural colours used in life-like images, such as people or landscapes, look more true to life when displayed at a colour temperature of 6500K. Black text on a white page is better represented by a colour temperature of 9300K.

Column is part of a memory array. A bit can be stored where a column and a row intersect.

COM Port is a connector that allow serial devices such as serial printers, modems, or mice to be connected to PC. Communication ports are also called serial ports. To keep track of the devices, the operating system assigns names such as such as COM1, COM2 etc.

Command is an instruction given to a computer. Also a key on a Mac called the Command Key and is used in some keyboard shortcuts.

Command Line Interface A command line interface (or CLI) is a text-based interface where the user types in various commands to execute tasks or run programs. Examples include MS-DOS Command Prompt, Windows PowerShell, MacOS Terminal, and Linux Terminal.

Command Mode is one of the two operating modes of the modem, sometimes called local mode or terminal mode. In command mode, the modem interprets any information it receives from the local computer (or terminal) as modem commands. It tries to perform the commands sent to it, and it returns result codes indicating the results of the commands. See also On-Line Mode.

Command Prompt is a command-line interpreter available in most operating systems such as Windows. On Unix-based systems (Linux/macOS), it's called a "terminal," "shell," or "command line".

CompactFlash or CF for short is a flash memory format introduced by SanDisk Corporation in 1994 widely used for digital devices and cameras.

Compact Disc is an optical storage medium developed by Sony and Phillips to store digital recordings and computer data.

The surface of the disc is marked with pits. This is how the data is encoded onto the disc.

Here we can see the inside of a CD drive.

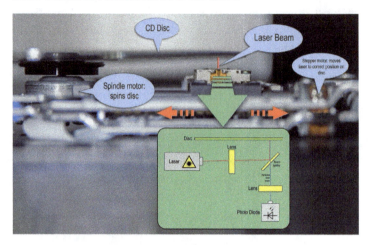

Comparison Operator is an operator often used in computer programming to compare two values.

Greater than	Greater than or equal to	Less than	Less than or equal to	Equal to
>	>=	<	<=	==

Compiler is a translation program that converts code written in a high level language such as C or C++ into machine code for execution on a computer.

Component Video carries a video signal (no audio) that has been split into three component channels: red, green, blue. It is often used to connect high end dvd players to televisions.

Composite Black is the colour back created from mixing cyan, magenta and yellow inks. Mixing inks is not a perfect operation, and composite black is often muddy. This is why the CMYK model is used in professional printing. See also True Black.

Composite Video is a video signal format that includes the complete visual waveform, including: chrominance (colour), luminance (brightness), blanking pedestal, field, line, colour sync pulses and field equalising pulses.

Compression is a data encoding technique used to reduce the amount of data for storage on a disk or transmission over a network. See lossless and lossy compression.

Content Management System (CMS) is a software application or a set of programs used to create, manage, modify, and publish digital content on the web. These systems provide a user-friendly interface that allows individuals or teams to collaboratively create and edit content without requiring technical expertise in web development or programming languages. Examples of popular CMS platforms include WordPress, Joomla, Drupal, and Shopify. CMSs play a crucial role in simplifying the process of content creation and management, empowering businesses and individuals to establish and maintain a dynamic online presence

Contone is short for continuous tone and is a technique used by colour printing technologies where each colour in the image is reproduced as a single tone. See Halftone

Contrast is the range between the lightest tones and the darkest tones in an image. The lower the number value, the more closely the shades will resemble each other. The higher the number, the more the shades will stand out from each other.

Control Unit is the component of a CPU that directs the operation of the processor as it executes instructions and creates control signals that tell the Arithmetic Logic Unit (ALU) and the Registers how to operate, what to operate on, and what to do with the result. The Control Unit makes sure everything happens in the right place at the right time.

Controller is the chip that translates computer data and instructions into a form suitable for use by a device such as a hard disk controller on an hard disk drive.

Controller Card is an expansion card that interprets the commands between the processor and the disk drive.

Convergence is the term used to describe how accurately the three (red, green, and blue) electron beams converge to illuminate their respective phosphors in a colour monitor.

Cookie is a small text file created by a website that is used to store the visiting user's preferences, location, and authenticate their session in order to tailor the experience to the user, or to track the user's use of the website. Session cookies are often used to track your movements such as the contents of your basket on an e-commerce site. Persistent cookies track your preferences on the website such as locale or language. Third party cookies collect data on your online movements, eg: what sites you've been on, or what you've been searching for, usually for the purpose of advertising.

CPPM is short for Content Copy Protection for Pre-recorded Media and was a digital copy protection system used for DVD-Audio discs. Developed when the intended CSS-II method of DVD-Audio encryption was abandoned after the emergence of the DeCSS hack.

CPRM is short for Content Protection for Recordable Media and was copy protection for writeable DVD formats that ensures the contents of the discs can't be copied.

CPU stands for Central Processing Unit and is a microprocessor chip that executes the instructions of a computer program. The AMD Phenom II and Intel Core i5 are examples of a CPU. The term sometimes also refers to the case that houses this chip. See also FPU.

CRC is short for Cyclic Redundancy Check and is a mathematical error checking technique where blocks of data get a short check value attached, commonly used in computer networks and storage devices.

Crossover Cable is a UTP cable usually used to connect network devices together directly. A commonly found version of this is called a half crossed cable, where the send/receive pairs are reversed on the other end.

Cryptocurrency refers to a type of digital or virtual currency that relies on cryptography for security and operates independently of a central authority, such as a government or financial institution. Eg: Bitcoin, Ethereum, Tether, Ripple and Polkadot

Cryptography is the practice and study of techniques used to secure communication and data from adversaries or malicious actors. It involves the creation and use of cryptographic algorithms to encrypt and decrypt information, ensuring confidentiality, integrity, and authenticity. Cryptography plays a crucial role in various applications, including securing online transactions, protecting sensitive data, and maintaining the privacy of communications. Common cryptographic techniques include encryption, hashing, digital signatures, and key management.

Crosstalk is interference from adjacent electronic circuitry or wire.

CRT is short for Cathode Ray Tube and is the large glass tube that made up older televisions or monitors in which rays of electrons were beamed onto a phosphorescent screen to produce images. Often still used as a generic term for a computer monitor.

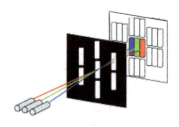

CSMA/CA Stands for Carrier Sense Multiple Access with Collision Avoidance and is a media access control protocol used on wireless networks that regulates data transmission over a shared channel. The sending host checks to see if the airway is free before sending. If the airway is free, the sending host sends a request to send signal (RTS). If there is no response to the RTS, then this means the receiving host is busy, so the sending host waits a random amount of time before trying again. If the sending host receives a clear to send signal (CTS), then it transmit its data.

CSMA/CD is short for Carrier Sense Multiple Access with Collision Detection and is a media access control protocol used in Ethernet technology for local area networking. The sending host checks to see if the line is free before sending. If the line is free, the sending host starts transmitting . If the line is not free then the sending host waits a random amount of time before trying again.

CSTN stands for Colour Super-Twist Nematic and is a passive matrix LCD technology developed by Sharp Electronics.

CTRL Key is a modifier key found on a keyboard used to execute keyboard shortcuts.

For example:
CTRL C = Copy
CTRL X = Cut
CTRL V = Paste

Cybernetics is an field that studies the control and communication processes in biological, mechanical, and electronic systems, aiming to understand how systems regulate themselves and interact with their environment.

Cybersecurity refers to the practice of protecting computer systems, networks, and data from unauthorized access, cyberattacks, and other digital threats. It encompasses a range of measures, technologies, and best practices aimed at safeguarding information assets and ensuring the confidentiality, integrity, and availability of data and resources. Cybersecurity efforts involve identifying potential vulnerabilities, implementing security controls and protocols, monitoring for suspicious activities, and responding to security incidents effectively. As the digital landscape evolves and cyber threats become more sophisticated, cybersecurity has become increasingly critical for organizations, governments, and individuals to mitigate risks and maintain trust in digital environments.

Cyberspace is a virtual computer world that allows users to communicate, share information, play games, and engage in social media.

Cylinder is a collection of tracks on multiple surfaces that are located at the same radius on each disk surface (ie concentric tracks).

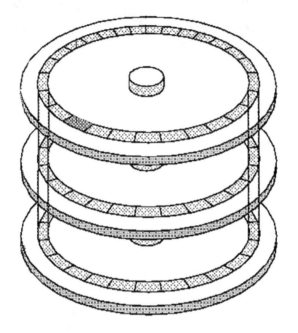

D

DAC stands for Digital-to-Analogue Converter and is a device (usually a single chip) that converts digital data into analogue signals. Graphics cards have traditionally required DACs to convert digital data to analogue signals that a monitor can process. Modems require a DAC to convert data to analogue signals that can be carried by telephone wires.

Daemon is a background process that runs on a Unix or Unix-like operating system, often starting at boot time to perform system tasks or wait for events to occur. Daemons are essential for server operations, handling tasks like network communications, file system monitoring, and security.

Database is a structured and organised collection of data. A common type is a relational database which is made up of tables with rows (records) containing fields of data indexed by a unique primary key. The database is searched or queried using a language called Structured Query Language. See DBMS, SQL.

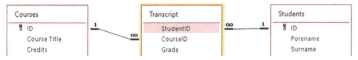

Data Bus is often used to transfer data to and from different components of a computer. This could be between the CPU and main memory or to another peripheral. The first standard data buses were 8-bit or 16-bit (early IBM PC), 32-bit came later in systems like the 80386 processor, whereas newer systems are 64-bit.

Data Cache is a temporary data store implemented using extremely fast RAM or on a disk drive that is used to store data so that subsequent requests for the data are served faster.

Data Compression is the encoding of text or data so that it takes up less space. Data compression allows more data to be stored on a disk to save space and is also used in data transmission so more data can be transmitted in a shorter period of time and thus increases its throughput. The data is decompressed by the receiver.

Data Link Layer is the second layer of the OSI (Open Systems Interconnection) seven layer reference model. It is responsible for establishing, maintaining, and terminating connections between devices on a local network, ensuring reliable and error-free transmission of data over the physical layer. The primary functions of the Data Link Layer include framing, addressing, error detection and correction, flow control, and media access control (MAC). It organizes data into frames, adds header and trailer information for transmission, and handles the physical addressing of devices on the network. Ethernet and Wi-Fi are examples of technologies that operate at the Data Link Layer.

Data Mining is the process of analyzing large sets of data to discover patterns, trends, and relationships that can inform decision-making. It involves the use of sophisticated data analysis tools to extract and identify useful information and knowledge from large databases.

Data Normalization is a process in database design that organizes tables and their relationships in a manner that reduces redundancy and dependency. It involves dividing large tables into smaller, less redundant tables without losing data integrity, to optimize database performance.

Data Structure is a specialized format for organizing, processing, retrieving, and storing data. It includes arrays, linked lists, stacks, queues, trees, and graphs, each designed for specific advantages in data management and algorithm efficiency.

Daughter Board is a printed circuit board that plugs into another larger circuit board such as a motherboard to extend its functionality.

DBMS is short for Database Management System is a piece of software that interacts with a user to capture and analyse data stored in a database. Examples include Microsoft Access, MySQL, Oracle.

DC is short for direct current and is an electrical current that travels in one direction often used to power a computer's electronic circuitry. Contrast with AC.

DCE is short for Data Circuit-terminating Equipment and is a device used to connect two DTEs over a network. Eg a modem.

D-Channel is an ISDN communication channel used for sending information between the ISDN equipment and the ISDN central office switch. The D-channel can also carry "user" packet data at rates up to 9.6 Kilobits.

DCT stands for Discrete Cosine Transform and is a coding methodology used in JPEG and MPEG image compression algorithms to reduce the number of bits for actual data compression. DCT converts data into sets of frequencies, the first being the most important. Latter frequencies are stripped away based on allowable resolution loss.

DDC stands for Display Data Channel. DDC 1/2B and 2AB are standardised techniques by which monitors and graphics cards communicate with each other to help establish the best resolution and refresh rate combination. DDC is only possible through a D-SUB connection.

DDE stands for Dynamic Data Exchange and is a system used in Windows to transfer data between two applications or two instances of the same application. DDE is also used to support OLE. See also OLE.

DDR stands for Double Data Rate and is a memory technology that works by allowing operations to occur on both the rising and falling edge of the clock cycle, thereby doubling the data transfer per clock cycle.

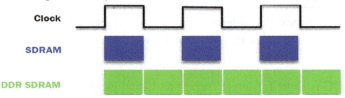

Deadlock in the context of an operating system is a situation where a resource required by a process is being held by another process, and vice versa.

Debug is the process of removing bugs or errors from a computer program.

Debugger is a development tool that allows a programmer to step through lines of code of a computer program in order to test and correct errors.

Decal is a texture that is placed specifically on one part of a 3D object.

Decimal or base 10 is the numbering system that uses 0, 1, 2, 3, 4, 5, 6, 7, 8, and 9.

Decision Tree is a model used in data mining for predictive modeling and machine learning. It represents decisions and their possible consequences, including chance event outcomes, resource costs, and utility. It's a way to display an algorithm that only contains conditional control statements.

Decode Unit decodes or translates complex machine language instructions into a simple format understood by the Arithmetic Logic Unit (ALU) and the Registers.

Decompression is to reverse the process used by the compression software algorithm to return data to its original size and condition.

DeCSS was an open-source Linux code that appeared in late 1990s that allowed encrypted DVD movies to be read.

Default is a predefined function or selection that is automatically selected by the computer unless the user specifies something else.

Default Gateway is the IP address of the router that connects a LAN to a wider network such as the internet. The IP address of the default gateway router is used to configure TCP/IP settings on machines connected to the LAN.

Defect Management is a technique ensuring long-term data integrity. Defect management consists of scanning disk drives both at the factory and during regular use, deallocating defective sectors before purchase and compensating for new defective sectors afterward.

Deflection Yoke is the arrangement of electromagnets which can alter the direction of the electron beam that passes through it.

Degauss in CRT monitors is the removal of the magnetic interference caused by a change in the position of the monitor in relation to the earth's magnetic field, or the presence of an artificial magnetic field that causes discolouration.

Delimiter is a character such as a comma(,) used to separate elements of data.

`Date,Name,Amount,Description`

Delta Frame also called difference frame is the frame in a video that contains only the pixels that are different from the preceding keyframe. Delta Frames reduce the overall size of the video clip to be stored on disk. See also Keyframe.

Denary is another word for decimal or base 10.

Density is a measure of how much substance there is in a given amount of space. Density = Mass divided by Volume.

Desktop Publishing or DTP for short is software such as Microsoft Publisher used to create print projects from business cards and flyers to magazines, books and posters. Many home DTP systems are affordable and designed to aid amateur level productions of common home printing tasks. More advanced DTP software packages such as Quark and InDesign are highly expensive and aimed at professional print designers.

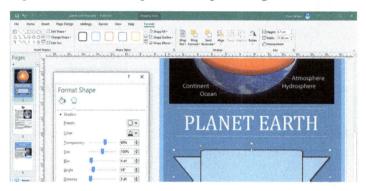

Device Driver is software often installed on an operating system that operates or controls a device such as a printer or video card, by providing a software interface to the hardware.

DFS stands for Distributed File System. It is a network file system that allows files, directories, and other resources to be shared and accessed across multiple computers or servers in a distributed environment. DFS provides a unified namespace and transparent access to files, regardless of their physical location or storage device. DFS is commonly used in enterprise environments to centralize file storage, facilitate collaboration among users, and improve data availability and reliability.

DHCP stands for Dynamic Host Configuration Protocol and is responsible for automatically allocating IP addresses to devices on a network. Devices connecting to a network broadcast a request to the DHCP server. The DHCP server sends back an IP address from its address pool along with a time period for which the allocation is valid called a lease, as well as DNS and gateway addresses, and the network's subnet mask.

DIB stands for Device-Independent Bitmap Format and was a common image format for Windows applications.

Die is an area of silicon containing an integrated circuit. A die has multiple layers, each with a specific function. A die refers to a semiconductor component or part that has not yet been packaged. The popular term for a die is chip.

Dielectric is a substance that is a poor conductor of electricity and will sustain the force of an electric field passing through it. Also called an insulator.

Diffuse Dither is a method for printing continuous-tone images on laser printers in which the greyscale information is represented by randomly located printer dots. Diffuse dithers do not photocopy well because of the small, random, dot location in the image.

Digital is a signal represented by turning a voltage on or off. Each on or off state represents a binary 1 or 0, respectively. Unlike analogue signals, digital signals can be repeatedly regenerated without introducing noise or distortion. See also Analogue.

Digital Certificate, also known as an SSL/TLS certificate or public key certificate, is a digital document issued by a trusted third-party certificate authority (CA) that verifies the identity of an entity, such as a website, server, organization, or individual, over the internet. Digital certificates contain information such as the entity's public key, identity information, expiration date, and the CA's digital signature, which serves as proof of the certificate's authenticity. Digital certificates are used in various security protocols, such as HTTPS (Hypertext Transfer

Protocol Secure), SSL/TLS (Secure Sockets Layer/Transport Layer Security), S/MIME (Secure/Multipurpose Internet Mail Extensions), and code signing, to establish encrypted connections, authenticate parties, and ensure data integrity and confidentiality in online communications and transactions.

Digital Signature is a means of verifying the authenticity of a digital message or document, often based on asymmetric cryptography.

Digital Video is a video signal represented by computer-readable binary numbers that describe a finite set of colours andluminance levels.

Digitisation is a process of transforming analogue signals into digital information.

DIMM stands for Dual In-line Memory Module and is a memory chip packaging that replaced the SIMM as the standard for PC memory, as unlike SIMMs, DIMMs don't have to be installed in pairs.

DIN Connector is a German standard used mostly for connecting keyboards, PS/2 style mice, MIDI, and Apple printer attachments.

Diode is an electronic component that acts primarily as a one-way valve.

DIP short for Dual In-Line Package and is chip housing with pins on each edge.

DIP Switch is a switch mounted on circuit board or device for configuring options.

Directory also commonly referred to as a folder, is a virtual container used for organizing and storing files and other directories within a file system. It acts as a hierarchical structure that allows users to categorize and manage their files in a logical manner. Directories can contain files, subdirectories, or both, and are often represented by names that reflect their contents or purpose. Users can navigate through directories to access and manipulate files, and directories are essential for maintaining order and facilitating efficient file management on computer systems.

DirecTV is an American direct broadcast satellite service provider owned by AT&T.

DirectX is an API used in Microsoft Windows, designed to provide software developers with direct access to low-level functions on a PC commonly used in games development.

Disk or sometimes Disc, is in general, any circular-shaped data-storage medium that stores data on the flat surface of the platter such as a magnetic disk in a hard disk drive or an optical disk in a CD, DVD or Bluray drive.

Disk Thrashing is a term that describes a hard disk drive that is constantly reading and writing data usually due to a lack of available RAM

Dithering is an image processing technique used to create the illusion of colour depth in images with a limited colour palette. For example a full-colour photograph can contain 16,777,216 colours.

Dithering is the most common method of reducing the colour range if you wanted to save the photograph as a GIF image which uses on 256 colours. The image below was converted from a full colour photograph to a 256 colour GIF.

DLL stands for Dynamic Link Library and is a packaged library containing functions that other programs can call, resources (such as icons) that other programs can use, or both. Unlike a standard programming library, whose functions are linked into an application when the application's code is compiled, an application that uses functions in a DLL links with those functions at runtime hence the term "dynamic".

Django is a high-level Python web framework that facilitates the rapid development of web applications. It follows the Model-View-Template (MVT) architectural pattern, providing developers with tools and utilities to streamline the creation of secure, maintainable, and scalable websites and web services. Key features of Django include an object-relational mapping (ORM) system for interacting with databases, a built-in administration interface, URL routing, a powerful template engine, authentication and authorization mechanisms, security features, and support for internationalization and localization. Django's design emphasizes simplicity, flexibility, and reusability, making it a popular choice for building complex web applications.

DLP stands for Digital Light Processor and is an all-digital display technology that turns image data into light. Enabled by a DMD device, DLP is capable of projecting sharp, clear images of almost any size without losing any of the original image's resolution.

DMA stands for Direct Memory Access and is a process by which data moves directly between a disk drive (or other device) and main memory (RAM) without the involvement of the CPU, thus allowing the system to continue processing other tasks while the new data is being retrieved.

DMD stands for Digital Micromirror Device and is an array of semiconductor-based digital mirrors that precisely reflect a light source for projection display and hard-copy applications. A DMD enables Digital Light Processing and displays images digitally. Rather than displaying digital broadcast signals as analogue signals, a DMD directs the digital signal directly to your screen.

DMT stands for Discrete Muliti Tone and is one of the two main modulation methods that can be used with ADSL technology. DMT divides the frequency spectrum supported by standard copper twisted-pair wire into 256 sub-frequencies from 64Khz to 1.1MHz.

DMZ Demilitarized Zone. In network security, a physical or logical subnetwork that contains and exposes an organization's external-facing services to an untrusted network, usually the Internet. The DMZ functions as a buffer zone between the public internet and the private internal network, adding an additional layer of security.

DNS stands for Domain Name System and is responsible for translating domain names into IP addresses. When you enter a URL into your browser, your computer will send the domain name (eg elluminetpress.com) to a DNS server. The DNS server responds with the IP address (eg 192.168.0.100). Your computer uses the IP address to connect to the web server.

DNS over HTTPS (DoH) is a protocol for performing remote Domain Name System (DNS) resolution via the HTTPS protocol. The goal of DoH is to increase user privacy and security by preventing eavesdropping and manipulation of DNS data 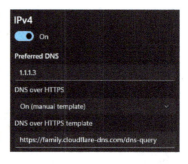 through man-in-the-middle attacks. By using HTTPS, DoH encapsulates DNS queries and responses within encrypted HTTP traffic. This ensures that DNS queries are secure, private, and cannot easily be blocked or tampered with by intermediaries.

DNS over TLS (DoT) is a security protocol for encrypting and wrapping Domain Name System (DNS) queries and responses over the Transport Layer Security (TLS) protocol. The primary purpose of DoT is to provide confidentiality and data integrity between the client and the DNS resolver. DoT encrypts DNS requests, protecting them from eavesdropping, tampering, and man-in-the-middle attacks. DoT operates on its designated port (853) to differentiate it from unencrypted DNS traffic.

DNSSEC (DNS Security Extensions) is a suite of Internet Engineering Task Force (IETF) specifications for securing certain kinds of information provided by the Domain Name System (DNS) as used on Internet Protocol (IP) networks. It is designed to protect the internet from certain attacks, such as DNS cache poisoning by ensuring the authenticity and integrity of DNS responses. DNSSEC adds digital signatures to DNS data to verify its authenticity, allowing clients to check the validity of the responses they receive. However, it does not encrypt data, meaning it does not provide confidentiality. DNSSEC aims to prevent attackers from redirecting traffic to malicious sites through DNS spoofing.

DNS Spoofing, short for Domain Name System Spoofing, is a type of cyber attack where the attacker forges or falsifies DNS records to redirect domain name resolutions to malicious IP addresses. By tampering with DNS responses, the attacker can redirect users to fake websites, intercept sensitive information, or disrupt network communications.

Dock In MacOS and iOS/iPadOS, the Dock is the row of app icons located across the bottom of the screen. The dock on a Mac in MacOS:

The dock on an iPad:

Dolby AC-3 is a perceptual digital audio coding technique capable of delivering multichannel digital surround sound. It incorporates 6 (5.1) discrete channels; each channel can carry a different signal simultaneously (left front, right front, centre, left rear, right rear, sub- woofer).

Dolby Digital is a digital audio encoding system from Dolby used in movie and home theatres that employs Dolby's AC-3 coding and compression technology to provide six channels of audio, known as 5.1 for front left, front right, front center, rear left, rear right and subwoofer.

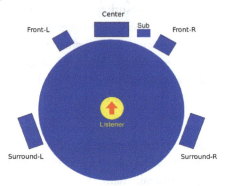

DOM (Document Object Model) is a programming interface provided by web browsers that represents the structure and content of HTML and XML documents as a hierarchical tree of objects. Each node in the tree corresponds to an element, attribute, or text content within the document.

The DOM provides methods and properties for developers to access, manipulate, and dynamically update the content and structure of web pages using scripting languages like JavaScript. It enables interactive web applications by allowing developers to respond to user actions, modify page elements, and update content dynamically without requiring a page reload.

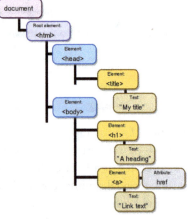

Domain (network administration). A domain refers to a group of devices or computers that share a common set of rules and policies within a local area network (LAN) or corporate network. A network domain typically includes a centralized server responsible for authentication, security, and resource management, such as a Windows Active Directory domain or a Linux domain using technologies like LDAP or NIS.

Domain (DNS) is a hierarchical naming system used to organize and identify resources connected to the internet. It consists of a series of labels separated by dots, with the top-level domain (TLD) appearing at the end (e.g., .com, .org, .net). Domains are used to assign human-readable names (domain names) to numerical IP addresses, allowing users to access websites, services, and other resources using easily recognizable names instead of complex IP addresses. See DNS.

Domain Name identifies a network domain, a resource, or a server hosting a website. The top-level domains such as .com, .co.uk, .edu, .gov, and .org are the highest level of domain names. Second-level domains commonly refer to the organization.

Each organization can also have sub-domains for different services such as website (www), mail servers (mail), or an e-commerce site (shop).

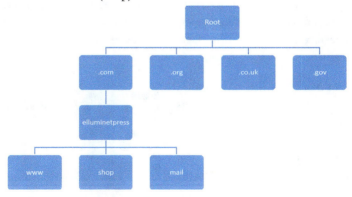

Doping is the introduction of an element that alters the conductivity of a semiconductor. Adding boron to silicon will create a P-type(more positive) material, while adding phosphorus or arsenic to silicon will create N-type (more negative) material.

DoS stands for Denial of Service. It is a type of cyber attack where the attacker seeks to disrupt the normal functioning of a target system or network by overwhelming it with a flood of illegitimate requests or traffic. Unlike DDoS attacks, which involve multiple compromised systems coordinating the attack, a DoS attack typically involves a single source flooding the target with traffic. The goal of a DoS attack is to render the target system or network inaccessible to legitimate users, causing disruption of service and potentially leading to financial losses or other negative impacts.

DOS stands for Disk Operating System. It refers to a family of operating systems that were prevalent in the early days of personal computing, primarily during the 1980s and early 1990s. One of the most famous versions of DOS is MS-DOS (Microsoft Disk Operating System), which was developed by Microsoft and became the standard operating system for IBM-compatible personal computers during that era. DOS provided a command-line interface for users to interact with the computer, manage files, and run programs. While DOS has largely been replaced by more modern operating systems with graphical user interfaces, its legacy continues to influence computing to this day.

Dot Matrix is a type of printer that uses one or two columns of dot hammers behind an ink ribbon to form text and images out of dots. The more dot hammers used, the higher the resolution of the printed image.

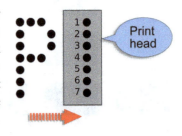

Dot Pitch is the distance between the centres of two same-colour phosphor dots on a CRT screen. The closer the dots, the smaller the dot pitch, and the sharper the image. See also Stripe Pitch.

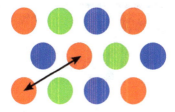

Dot Trio is the standard triad arrangement of the three primary colours on a screen.

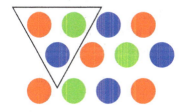

DPMS stands for Display Power Management Signalling and is a monitor that comply with this can be managed by Power Management features found in CMOS configuration on Energy Saving PCs.

DQM Data Mask is the control signal used by SDRAMs to provide byte masking during read and write operations. There is one DQM signal for every 8 bits of data width.

DRAM stands for Dynamic Random Access Memory and is the memory used to store data in personal computers. DRAM stores each bit of information in a cell composed of a capacitor and a transistor. Because the capacitor in a DRAM cell can hold a charge for only a few milliseconds, DRAM must be continually refreshed in order to retain its data. See also EDO RAM and SRAM.

DRDRAM stands for Direct Rambus DRAM and is a RAM architecture developed by Rambus in the 1990s through to the early-2000s.

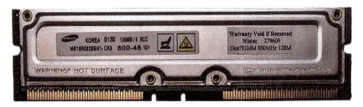

Drive Bay refers to a compartment within a computer's case designed to accommodate disk drives. These bays are typically 5.25 inches or 3.5 inches wide, to match the form factor of the drives being installed. Drive bays can be designed for internal access, concealing devices like hard drives within the computer case, or for external access, allowing for the insertion and removal of media in devices like DVD-ROM drives.

Drive Geometry describes the physical layout of a disk drive, specifically the number of heads (the read/write mechanisms), cylinders (concentric tracks formed by the platters), and sectors per track (divisions of each track where data is stored). This geometry is crucial for understanding the storage capacity and organization of a disk drive.

Driver is a specialized software program that enables communication between the operating system and hardware devices, such as graphics cards, printers, scanners, or other peripherals. Manufacturers develop drivers to ensure their hardware devices can operate effectively with various operating systems, providing necessary instructions for the device's operations and functionalities.

Digital Rights Management (DRM) encompasses a series of access control technologies to restrict the usage of digital content and devices post-purchase. DRM aims to prevent unauthorized distribution and use of copyrighted digital media.

DSP stands for Digital Signal Processor and is an electronic device designed to convert an analogue signal into a digital data stream (and vice-versa). DSPs are used in a variety of devices such as personal computers, high speed modems, sound cards, and real-time audio/video compression and decompression hardware.

DSP Solution is the use of a Digital Signal Processor in conjunction with mixed-signal devices and embedded software to collect, process, compress, transmit and display the analogue and digital data found in today's most popular multimedia applications.

DSS stands for Digital Satellite System, a network of satellites that broadcast digital data. An example of a DSS is DirecTV, which broadcasts digital television signals.

DSSS stands for Direct-Sequence Spread Spectrum and is one of two types of spread spectrum radio that continuously changes frequencies or signal patterns. DSSS multiplies the data bits by a very fast pseudo-random bit pattern that "spreads" the data into a large coded stream that takes the full bandwidth of the channel.

D-SUB Connector is a common "D" shaped electrical connector used to connect computer peripherals together such as monitors or serial devices. A common D-Sub connector was used to connect a monitor to a PC. Below: serial and VGA

DTCP stands for Digital Transmission Content Protection and is a system devised for secure transmission in the home environment over two-way transmission lines such as the FireWire bus. DTCP prevents unauthorised copying of digital content while allowing legitimate copying for purposes such as time shifting.

DTE stands for Data Terminal Equipment and is an end device on a communications circuit such as a PC or workstation.

DTR stands for Data Transfer Rate and is the speed at which data is transferred between a host and a data recording device. Usually noted in KBps or MBps, and sometimes in MB/minute. Can mean a "peak" rather than a "sustained" transfer rate.

Dual boot is the process of setting up a computer to run two different operating systems (OS) on the same device, allowing users to choose between them during the boot process. This configuration enables users to have access to multiple operating systems on a single computer and switch between them.

To set up a dual boot configuration, users typically partition their hard drive or use separate physical drives for each operating system. During the boot process, the system presents a boot menu, allowing users to select the desired operating system to load. Each OS installation remains isolated from the other, preserving their respective settings, applications, and data.

Duplex is a point to point communication system that allows two or more devices to communicate. Half duplex transmissions, only one device can send data at a time. Full duplex transmissions allow both devices to send data at the same time.

DV is a consumer digital video format that uses 1/4" (6.35mm) metal evaporated tape, recorded at 25 Mbps on MiniDV cassettes providing up to 90 minutes of record time in long-play mode.

DVB stands for Digital Video Broadcasting project and is a European consortia that developed a set of standards that define digital broadcasting using existing satellite, cable, and terrestrial transmission. See also ATSC.

DVD (Digital Versatile Disc or Digital Video Disc) is a type of optical disk technology similar to the compact disc (CD) but with a much higher data storage capacity. DVDs are used for storing digital video, audio, and computer data. The standard single-layer DVD can hold 4.7GB of data. Dual-layer DVDs offer even higher capacities, up to 8.5GB.

DVDs come in different formats, including DVD-ROM (read-only memory), DVD-R and DVD+R (recordable), DVD-RW and DVD+RW (rewritable), and DVD-Video and DVD-Audio for specific content playback.

The DVD format has been widely used for home entertainment and data storage, although it has been superseded by Blu-ray Discs.

Here we can see the inside of a DVD drive

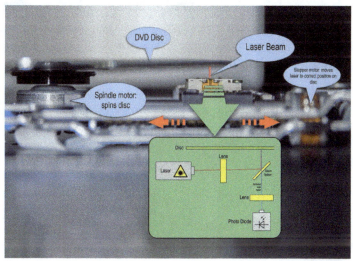

Here is a view from the top of the drive

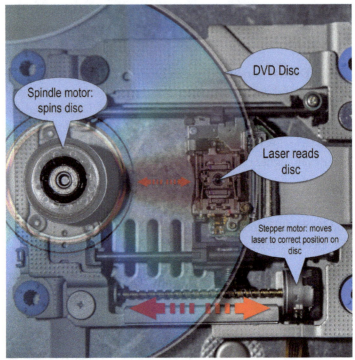

DVD-Audio is the DVD audio-only storage format similar to CD- Audio. DVD-Audio is facing stiff competition from a number of other high fidelity audio standards.

DVI is a digital interface for connecting to computer monitors and projectors. There are three types DVI-I, DVI-D and DVI-A.

DVI-A short for DVI-Analog and is an analog only format that supports resolutions of up to 1920x1200.

DVI-D short for DVI-Digital only carries digital signals and can be dual or single link. DVI-D supports resolutions of up to 1920x1200 single link, or 2560x1600 dual link.

DVI-I Single Link. DVI cable with integrated analog for both analog and digital displays up to 1920 × 1200

DVI-I Dual Link. DVI cable with integrated analog for both analog and digital displays up to 2560 × 1600

DVI-I short for DVI-Integrated supports both digital and analog signals and can be dual or single link. DVI-I supports resolutions of up to 1920x1200 single link, or 2560x1600 dual link.

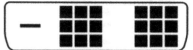

DVI-D Digital Single Link. DVI cable with digital signal only for displays up to 1920 × 1200

DVI-D Digital Dual Link. DVI cable with digital signal only for displays up to 2560 × 1900

Dye-Sublimation is a specialist print technology used for demanding graphic arts and photographic applications that require continuous tone output.

Dynamic DNS (DDNS) is a service that automatically updates the DNS records of a domain name with the current IP address of a device, typically a computer or network device, whose IP address changes frequently. This allows the device to be accessible via a domain name, even if its IP address changes due to factors such as DHCP (Dynamic Host Configuration Protocol) lease expiration or network reconfiguration. DDNS is commonly used in scenarios where hosting servers or accessing devices with dynamic IP addresses need to maintain a consistent hostname for remote access or service availability.

Dynamic Disk is a feature in Windows operating systems that allow a user to resize a volume or to span it across multiple drives. Dynamic disks can be also be striped or mirrored to provide performance gains and fault tolerance.

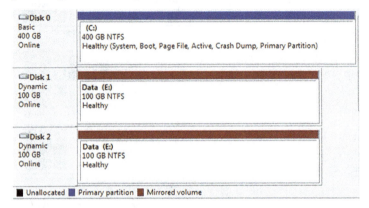

Dynamic Linking refers to the process of linking a program to its libraries at runtime rather than at compile time. Dynamic linking allows a program to call external functions or procedures, which are located in separate files or libraries, without being explicitly embedded within the executable file.

Dynamic Power Management Architecture is Intel's power optimization framework that dynamically adjusts power consumption based on workload demands to enhance efficiency and performance while reducing energy usage..

E

E1 is a four-wire European telephone company standard that carries data at 2.048 Mbit/s, equivalent of a US T1 line.

EAX stands for Environmental Audio Extensions and is a now deprecated hardware and software audio standard developed by Creative Labs, used originally in the SoundBlaster cards.

ECC stands for Error Correction Code and is a system used to detect errors that can be corrected by the device's controller when the data is read. See also CRC.

ECMA stands for European Computer Manufacturers Association and is a non-profit international industry association founded in 1961 dedicated to the worldwide standardisation of information and communication systems.

EDAP stands for Extended Data Availability and Protection and was Created by the RAID Advisory Board in 1997.

EDGE stands for Enhanced Data for GSM Evolution and is a mobile phone technology that was developed as an extension to GSM that allows improved data rates.

EDO DRAM stands for Extended Data Out Random Access Memory and is a form of DRAM that has a two-stage pipeline, allowing the memory controller to read data while it is being reset for the next operation.

EDP stands for Enhanced Dot Pitch and is Hitachi's tube technology in which the phosphor triads are spaced closer together horizontally than they are vertically.

EDRAM stands for Enhanced Dynamic Random Access Memory and is a form of DRAM that boosts performance by placing a small complement of static RAM (SRAM) in each DRAM chip and using the SRAM as a cache. Also known as cached DRAM, or CDRAM.

EDVAC stands for Electronic Discrete Variable Automatic Computer and was the first computer to incorporate Von Neumann's stored program concept, in which the programme executed by the computer was stored as data, rather than existing as wire connections. Designed in 1946, when EDVAC became fully operational in 1952 it contained approximately 4,000 vacuum tubes and 10,000 crystal diodes.

EEPROM stands for Electrically Erasable Programmable Read Only Memory: a special type of read-only memory (ROM) that can be erased and written electrically. EEPROM maintains its contents without power backup and is frequently used for system-board BIOS's.

EGA is IBM's standard for colour displays prior to the VGA standard. It specified a resolution of 640×350 with up to 16 colours and a 9-pin (DB-9) connector.

EIA stands for Electronic Industries Association: a trade association representing the U.S. high technology community which began life in 1924 as the Radio Manufacturers Association. It has been responsible for developing some important standards, such as the RS-232, RS-422 and RS-423 standards for connecting serial devices. In 1988, it spun off its Information & Telecommunications Technology Group into a separate organisation known as the TIA.

EIDE stands for Enhanced Integrated Device Electronics or Enhanced Intelligent Drive Electronics: an enhanced version of the IDE drive interface that expands the maximum disk size from 504Mb to 8.4Gb, more than doubles the maximum data transfer rate, and supports up to four drives per PC (as opposed to two in IDE systems). EIDE's primary competitor is SCSI-2, which also supports large hard disks and high transfer rates.

EISA stands for Extended Industry Standard Architecture: an open 32-bit extension to the ISA 16-bit bus standard designed by Compaq, AST and other clone makers in response to IBM's proprietary MCA (Micro Channel Architecture) 32-bit bus design. Unlike the Micro Channel, an EISA bus is backward-compatible with 8-bit and 16-bit expansion cards designed for the ISA bus.

EIST stands for Enhanced Intel Speed Step technology: an enhanced version of Intel's Speed Step technology which dynamically scales the speed of a processor between its default clock setting and a minimum speed, based on how much CPU horsepower is needed at that moment, so as to both reduce power consumption and heat.

EM64T is short for Extended Memory 64 Technology: an enhancement to Intel's IA-32 architecture which allows a processor to run newly written 64-bit code and access larger amounts of memory when used with a 64-bit OS and application. These extensions do not run code written for the Intel Itanium processor.

Embedded Servo is the device some disk drives use to move the head a tracks.

Embedded System is a computer control system that is built into a device such as the control system in a car, washing machine or a microwave oven.

113

Emoji

Emoji is a small digital image or icon used to express an idea, emotion, or concept in electronic communications. Emojis are widely used in messaging, social media, and various forms of digital communication to enhance the expression of feelings, attitudes, or reactions, often in a more efficient or playful way than text alone can convey.

Emoticon combination of characters, typically punctuation marks and letters, used to represent facial expressions, gestures, or emotions in text-based communication. Emoticons are commonly employed in messaging, emails, social media posts, and online forums to convey tone and mood, adding nuance and context to written messages. Examples of emoticons include :-) for a smiley face, :-(for a frown, ;-) for a wink, and :-D for laughter. Emoticons are often considered a precursor to modern emojis, which are graphical representations of emotions and objects used in digital communication.

Encoding is the process of converting data into another form. Digital video from a camera can be encoded using H264 or MPEG, an image from a camera can be encoded using JPEG. Characters on a keyboard can be encoded in binary using ASCII.

Encryption is a method used to convert data into an unrecognisable form using a cryptographic key.

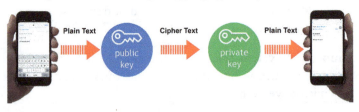

Energy Star launched in 1993, this is a program established by the Environmental Protection Agency (EPA) as a partnership with the computer industry to promote the introduction of energy-efficient personal computers which help reduce air pollution caused by power generation. To comply with the Energy Star guidelines, a computer system or monitor must consume less than 30 watts of power in its lowest power state.

EPP stands for Enhanced Parallel Port: a parallel port that conforms to the EPP standard developed by the IEEE 1284 standards committee. The EPP specification transforms a parallel port into an expansion bus that can handle up to 64 disk drives, tape drives, CD-ROM drives, and other mass-storage devices.

EPROM is short for Erasable Programmable Read Only Memory and is a memory chip that can store programs and data in a non-volatile state, meaning the chip retains the memory when the power is cut. These devices are erased by high-intensity ultraviolet (UV) light and can then reprogrammed.

Error is an unexpected result due to a bug or flaw in a program or a hardware fault

Error Control is the encoding of text or data so that a receiver can detect and correct errors in data transmissions.

Error Message is a message displayed to the user when a problem or fault occurs.

eSATA cables connect to some types of high speed external portable hard drives. The eSATA cable cannot transmit power, unless you use eSATAp (powered eSATA).

Escape Sequence is a sequence of three characters (normally "+++") that switches the modem from the on-line mode to the command mode without breaking the telephone connection.

ESCD is a region of non-volatile memory used by BIOS and ICU (Intel Configuration Utility) or PnP operating system to record information about the current configuration of the system.

ESDI stands for Enhanced Small Device Interface: an interface standard developed by a consortium of the leading PC manufacturers for connecting disk drives to PCs. Introduced in the early 1980s, ESDI was two to three times faster than the older ST-506 standard. It has long since been superseded by the IDE, EIDE and SCSI interfaces.

Etch is a process using a chemical bath (wet etch) or a plasma (dry etch) that removes unwanted substances from the wafer surface.

Ethernet is a networking technology used to connect computers and devices together and is commonly used in LANs. Ethernet can transfer data at 100Mbps on some cables and 1Gbps – 10Gbps on high speed cables.

Ethernet Switch is a multiport layer 2 hardware device that connects devices such as PCs, Wireless APs, servers, or printers to a computer network.

ETSI stands for European Telecommunications Standards Institute: a non- profit membership organisation founded in 1988, dedicated to standardising telecommunications throughout Europe. It promotes worldwide standards, and its efforts are co-ordinated with the ITU.

Exception refers to an anomalous or unexpected event that occurs during the execution of a program, disrupting the normal flow of execution. Exceptions can arise due to errors, faults, or exceptional conditions such as division by zero, invalid memory access, or file not found. Exception handling mechanisms in programming languages allow developers to detect, handle, and recover from such exceptions, preventing program crashes and ensuring robustness.

Execute refers to the process of carrying out or performing a program, task, or instruction on a computer system. When a program is executed, the instructions it contains are sequentially interpreted and processed by the computer's central processing unit (CPU) or other processing units, resulting in the execution of specific operations and the generation of desired outcomes.

exFAT is short for Extensible File Allocation Table and is a file system optimized for USB flash drives, external hard drives, and memory cards. exFAT has a maximum volume size of 128PB, and a maximum file size of 16 EB. This is a useful file format for formatting external drives as it provides compatibility across different operating systems such as Windows and MacOS.

Expansion Bus is an input/output bus typically comprised of a series of slots on the motherboard. Expansion boards are plugged into the bus. ISA, EISA, PCI express and VL-Bus are examples of expansion buses used in a PC.

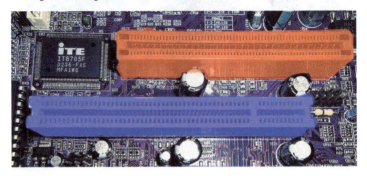

Expansion Card is a circuit board that fits into a computer expansion slot to add a certain function (like a modem, sound card, or SCSI interface).

Expert System An artificial intelligence (AI) system designed to emulate the decision-making ability and problem-solving skills of human experts in a specific domain or field. Expert systems use knowledge representation techniques to capture and formalize expert knowledge, which is then used by an inference engine to make decisions or provide recommendations based on input data or user queries.

These systems typically consist of a knowledge base containing domain-specific information and rules, along with an inference engine that applies reasoning mechanisms to derive conclusions or solutions.

Expert systems are utilized in various domains, including healthcare, finance, engineering, and customer support, to assist users in making complex decisions, diagnosing problems, troubleshooting issues, and providing expert advice. They are often employed in situations where human expertise is scarce or costly to access, enabling organizations to leverage existing knowledge and expertise efficiently.

Export commonly refers to the process of saving or converting data in a particular format or file type that can be used by other software applications or systems.

External Hard Drive is an external hard drive is a permanent storage device that sits outside a computer and is usually connected using a USB cable.

F

FAQ stands for Frequently Asked Questions and as its name suggests is a list of questions and answers that are most commonly asked by customers or users of a system or product.

FAT stands for File Allocation Table and is the file system used by MS-DOS and Windows to manage and store files on a hard disks, external hard disk, memory card of flash drive. The file system takes its name from an on-disk data structure known as the file allocation table, which records where individual portions of each file are located on the disk.

FAT16 is a file system used in early versions of Windows. FAT16 had a maximum volume size of 2GB, and a maximum file size of 2GB.

FAT32 is a file system used in Windows 98, which supports larger partition sizes and smaller cluster sizes than FAT16, thereby improving disk performance and increasing available disk space. FAT32 supports a theoretical maximum volume size of 16TB, but Windows' built-in formatter limits it to 32GB. The maximum file size for FAT32 is 4GB.

FCC stands for Federal Communications Commission and is the U.S. Government agency that supervises, licenses, and regulates electronic and electromagnetic transmission standards.

FCPGA stands for Flip Chip Plastic Grid Array and is a micro CPU package, for socketable boards, consisting of a die placed face-down on an organic substrate. The package uses 478 pins, which are 2.03 mm long and .32 mm in diameter.

FDD or floppy disk drive, is a storage device that reads and writes data to floppy disks.

FDDI is an ANSI standard for high-speed networking that uses a dual-ring topology with fiber optic cabling, supporting speeds of 100 Mbps over distances of up to two kilometers. Typically used as backbones for wide area networks (WANs).

FDMA stands for Frequency Division Multiple Access and is a mobile communications technique in which the radio spectrum is divided into frequency bands.

Feathering is a term used when describing printed text quality. Feathering occurs when deposited ink follows the contours of the paper. Depending on the viscosity of the ink, the rougher the grain of the paper the more pronounced the feathering will be.

FED stands for Field Emission Display: a display technology which use vacuum tubes (one for each pixel) with conventional RGB phosphors.

Fetch Execute Cycle is the basic operating cycle used by the CPU to retrieve or fetch and instruction from memory, then decode and execute it.

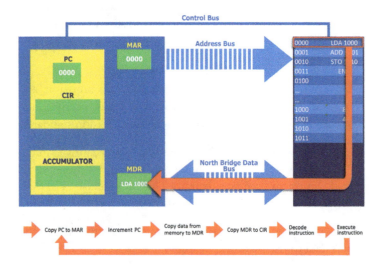

FHSS stands for Frequency Hopping Spread Spectrum and is radio transmission method that continuously changes the Centre frequency of a carrier several times per second according to a pseudo-random set of channels, thereby making illegal monitoring extremely difficult, if not impossible. See also DSSS.

Fiber is a long distance medium for telecommunications and computer data networking where data is transmitted by sending pulses of infrared light through the optical fiber.

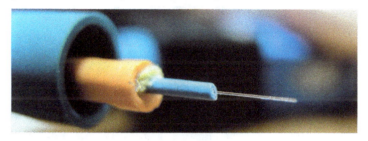

Fiber-optic Communication is a method of transmitting data by sending pulses of infrared light through a fiber optic cable.

Field is a data unit found on a table in a database used to store a value such as a name. Also an element on a user interface designed to accept data from a user such as a search field on a web page.

FIFO stands for First In-First Out and is a storage method that retrieves the item stored for the longest time (ie the first item in). See also LIFO.

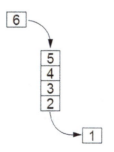

File is an object that contains data. A file can be a Word document, a photograph, a video, audio, or music.

File Explorer formerly known as Windows Explorer, is an app used for browsing and managing files in Windows 10/11. You'll find the icon on the taskbar.

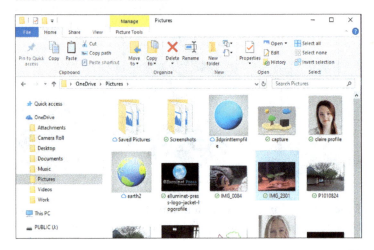

File Server is a computer on a network that provides devices access to centralised shared files.

File System specifies how data is organised and stored on a storage medium such as a hard disk drive. File systems are usually hierarchical meaning the data is organised allowing the user to organise their files into directories or folders. Common examples are: NTFS on Windows, HFS or APFS on a Mac, or EXT on linux

File Transfer Protocol is a protocol used for transferring files to and from a remote machine usually over port 21. FTP either runs in active or passive mode. In active mode, the client opens a port on the local machine. Once the client issues a command to transfer a file, the server connects to the port on the client. In passive mode the client initiates both sides of the connection. When the client issues a command to transfer a file, the client establishes a connection to the server. Passive mode is the most common.

Fill Factor is used in connection with digital display technologies (such as LCD and DLP) to convey how much of the area of a single pixel is used for the image as opposed to the grid surrounding the pixel. The higher the "fill factor" the better. See also Screen Door Effect.

Filtering is a process used in both analogue and digital image processing to reduce bandwidth. Filters can be designed to remove information content such as high or low frequencies, for example, or to average adjacent pixels, creating a new value from two or more pixels.

Finder is a file management app used on the Apple Macintosh computers. You'll find the finder app located on the bottom left of the dock.

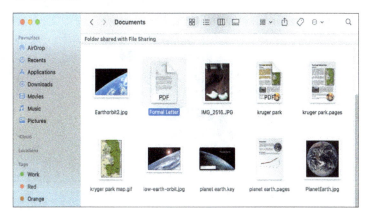

Firewall is a hardware device or computer program that resides between an internal network or computer and the Internet. It can be configured to allow only specific kinds of messages from the Internet to pass to the internal network, thereby protecting it from intruders or hackers who might try to use the Internet to break into those systems.

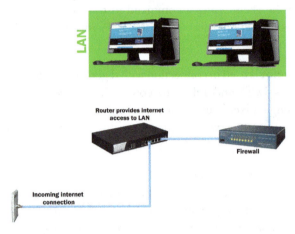

FireWire also known as IEEE 1394 or iLink and is a high speed serial-bus standard for transferring video, audio and data through a universal I/O interface in a similar fashion to USB. This technology was often used in digital cameras, CD/DVD drives, hard disk drives and some audio equipment. FireWire 400 and FireWire 800 ran at 400 and 800 Mbps.

Later standards such as S1600 and S3200 transferred data at 1.5Gbps to 3Gbps.

126

Firmware is a program loaded directly into a ROM or EEPROM chip for controlling the operation of the computer or peripheral devices. Distinct from software, which is stored in read/write memory and can be altered.

Fixed Point Number is a number that has a fixed number of digits after the decimal point.

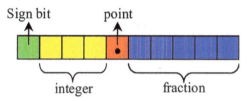

Flash Drive is a data storage device that uses flash memory to store data and can be plugged into a USB port.

Flash Memory is a non-volatile memory device that retains its data when the power is removed. The device is similar to EPROM with the exception that it can be electrically erased, whereas an EPROM must be exposed to ultra-violet light to erase. Commonly used in digital cameras.

Flash ROM is a type of memory used for firmware in modems and other digital devices. Unlike conventional ROM (read-only memory), flash ROM can be erased and reprogrammed, making it possible to update a product's firmware without re-placing memory chips.

Flat Panel Display is a thin display screen that uses any of a number of technologies, such as LCD, plasma and FED. Traditionally used in laptops, flat panel displays are slowly beginning to replace desktop CRTs for specialised applications.

Flat Shading is the simplest form of 3D shading which fills polygons with one colour. Processor overheads are negligible and 3D games will allow the graphics to be stripped down to flat shading to improve the frame rate.

Float is short for floating-point number, is a data type used in computing to represent numbers with fractional parts. Floats are characterized by their ability to store numbers with a decimal point and can represent a wide range of values, including both very large and very small numbers.

Floating Point numbers are those that contain floating decimal points such as 88.87, 955.35, 0.06.

For example, the number 454.75 can be expressed as

$$4.5475 * 10^2$$

4.5475 is called the mantissa. The 2 is the exponent (this tells you where to move the decimal point), and 10 is the number base (in this case decimal base 10). Similarly 0.0025 can be expressed as

$$2.5 * 10^{-3}$$

Floppy Drive is somewhat obsolete nowadays and was included in most PCs. The 3.5in high density floppy disk could hold 1.44MB of data. Older floppy disks were 5.25in disks.

128

Flow Control refers to techniques and mechanisms employed in computer networking and communication systems to manage the flow of data between sender and receiver, ensuring efficient and reliable transmission. Also in computer programming, statements used to control flow of program such as IF statements, FOR and WHILE loops.

Flux Density is the number of magnetic field patterns that can be stored on a given area of disk surface, used as a measure of data density. The number is usually stated as flux changes per inch (FCI), with typical values in the tens of thousands.

Fly Height is the distance between the read/write head and the disk surface. A cushion of air keeps the head from hitting the surface of the disk. Smaller fly heights allow denser data storage but require more precise mechanics.

FM is short for Frequency Modulation and is a data transmission technique that encodes the data by varying (or modulating) the frequency of the carrier wave.

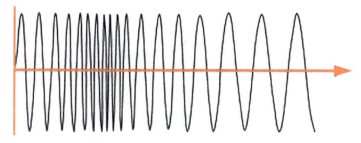

Font is a typeface of a specific point size, weight and style. For example: Times New Roman is a typeface. **Times New Roman Bold**, Times New Roman Regular, or *Times New Roman Italic* are all fonts.

Folder also known as a directory, is a virtual container used to organize and store files and other folders within a file system or operating system environment

For Loop is a flow control statement is a programming language used to execute a section of code repeatedly for a set number of times. For example, reading items in a list using Python.

```
cars = ["merc", "bmw", "audi"]
for x in cars:
    print(x)
```

Form Factor is the size, shape, and physical arrangement of computer components such as motherboards, add on cards, power supplies, disk drives and so on. The physical size of a device as measured by outside dimensions. With regard to a disk drive, the form factor is the overall diameter of the platters and case, such as 3.5in or 5.25in, not the size in terms of storage capacity. If the drive is a 5.25in form factor it means that the drive is the same size as a 5.25in diskette drive and uses the same fixing points.

Format is a process of preparing a storage medium such as a hard disk drive for an operating system to store data using a file system such as NTFS, FAT32 or exFAT.

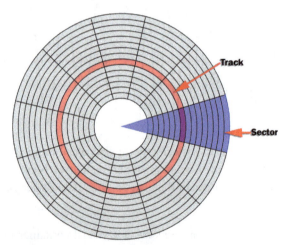

Also the way in which something is arranged or set out such as a document format

Formatted Capacity is the amount of space left to store data on a disk after writing the sector headers, boundary definitions, and timing information during a format operation. The size of a drive always is reported in formatted capacity, accurately reflecting the usable space available.

FPM DRAM stands for Fast Page Mode RAM and is a timing option that permits several bits of data in a single row on a DRAM chip to be accessed at an accelerated rate. FPM DRAM optimizes memory access by keeping a row address active, allowing multiple column accesses within the same row before needing to refresh.

FPS stands for Frames Per Second and is the number of frames shown in each second of time.

FPU is short for Floating Point Unit and is a part of the computer's CPU that performs floating point calculations. See Floating Point.

Fractals are never-ending repeating patterns such as the Mandelbrot Set

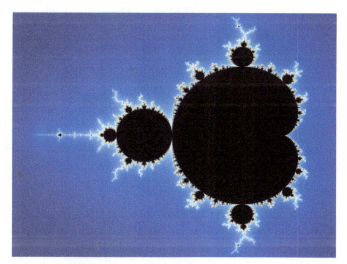

Frame is a single, complete picture in a video. Also a unit of data transmission on a computer network.

Frame Buffer is a buffer often used in display memory that temporarily stores a full frame of picture at one time.

Frame Grabber is a device that captures a frame from a full motion video.

Frame Rate is how many frames a screen displays in one second. NTSC shows 30 frames per second. PAL is 25 frames per second.

Front Projection is when a projector is positioned in front of the screen. See also Rear Projection.

Front Side Bus is the data bus that connects the CPU to the main memory (RAM).

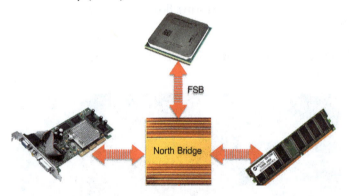

FSK is a modulation technique where data is encoded by shifting the frequency of a carrier wave between two distinct values, commonly used in modems and RFID systems..

FST is short for Flat Square Tube and describes the viewing surface of a cathode ray tube that is nearly flat. Flatter screens give the appearance of straighter lines, and they can aid in the reduction of glare, compared to conventional tubes.

FTP stands for File Transfer Protocol and is a protocol for transferring files to and from a remote machine usually over port 21. FTP either runs in active or passive mode. In active mode, the client opens a port on the local machine. Once the client issues a command to transfer a file, the server connects to the port on the client. In passive mode the client initiates both sides of the connection. When the client issues a command to transfer a file, the client establishes a connection to the server. Passive mode is the most common.

FTTC stands for Fibre to the Cabinet. The fibre optic cable runs from the exchange to the telephone cabinet in your street and uses vDSL over the copper phone line to run the last 100-300m or so to your house.

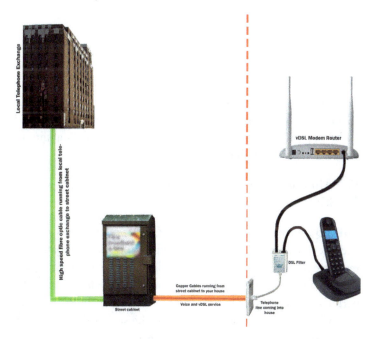

FTTP stands for Fibre to the Premises. The fibre optic cable runs from the telephone exchange to the socket on the wall in your house. The fibre optic cable will plug into a modem supplied by your ISP which will connect you to the internet.

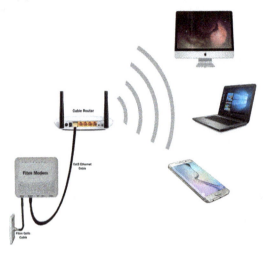

Full-Duplex is often used in reference to communications channels or devices and means that data can be sent and received at the same time. Also used to describe a soundcard's ability to record and playback digital audio at the same time.

Full-Motion Video is video shown at 29.97 frames per second (NTSC), 25 frames per second.

Fully Qualified Domain Name (FQDN) refers to a complete and specific domain name that provides the absolute path to a resource on the internet. An FQDN includes the host name, any subdomains, and the top-level domain (TLD), all separated by periods. For example, "www.example.com" is an FQDN where "www" is the host name, "example" is the second-level domain, and ".com" is the TLD. FQDNs are essential for accurately identifying and accessing resources on the internet, ensuring precise routing and resolution of network requests.

G

Gain is the increase in signalling power as an audio signal is boosted by an electronic device. It is measured in decibels.

Gamma is a mathematical curve representing both the contrast and brightness of an image. Moving the curve in one direction will make the image darker and decrease the contrast. Moving the curve the other direction will make the image lighter and increase the contrast.

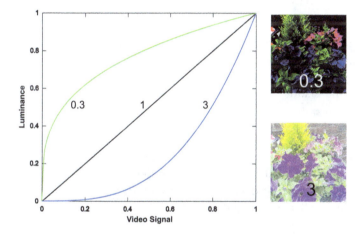

Gamma Correction is used to correct the differences between the way a camera captures an image and the way a monitor displays the image in order to display the image accurately.

Gamut is the range of colours that can be captured or represented by a device.

Gateway is a hardware device that serves as a bridge between two different types of network and that contains the necessary protocol translation software to enable them to exchange information. The router that your ISP sends you acts as a gateway between your home network and the internet.

GB stands for Gigabyte, a unit of data storage equivalent to 1 billion bytes (1,073,741,824 bytes).

GBps stands for GigaBytes per second, a data rate used to measure the speed of a network or, mass storage devices and memory systems.

GDI short for Graphical Device Interface, a component of Windows that allows applications to draw on screens, printers, and other output devices. A GDI compliant printer will print exactly what is displayed on a Windows screen without having to transpose it into a printer.

General MIDI is a table of 128 standard sounds or instruments for MIDI cards and synthesisers.

Gflops is short for Gigaflops equalling 1 thousand million floating-point opeartions per second.

Ghosting is a visual artifact in LCD screens where fast-moving objects leave behind a faint trail or blur due to slow pixel response times. The term 'ghosting' is also informally used to describe cutting off communication with someone without warning.

GiB stands for Gibibyte and is a unit of measure consisting of 1024MiB.

GIF is short for Graphics Interchange Format and is an image limited to 256 colours with transparency commonly found on the web.

Gigabit Ethernet is a version of Ethernet that runs at 1Gbps.

Git is a distributed version control system used for tracking changes in source code during software development.

GNU (GNU's Not Unix) an extensive project initiated in 1983 by Richard Stallman with the aim to develop a free Unix-like operating system. The project's name, "GNU's Not Unix," is a recursive acronym, highlighting its design to be fully compatible with Unix but entirely free software. The GNU project has been instrumental in the free software movement, advocating for the freedoms to use, study, modify, and distribute software. Its contributions include not only the development of software tools and applications that form part of the GNU operating system but also the creation of the GNU General Public License (GPL). The GPL is a widely adopted free software license that ensures users can freely modify and share software licensed under it. While the GNU project itself does not include the Linux kernel, the combination of GNU tools and the Linux kernel has resulted in the widely used GNU/Linux operating system.

GPF stands for General Protection Fault is a type of error that occurs within an operating system when a program attempts to access a region of memory that is not allowed, or tries to perform an operation that is not permitted. This can happen for a variety of reasons including accessing invalid memory addresses, executing non-executable memory, or when software tries to write to read-only memory. GPFs are most commonly associated with the Microsoft Windows operating systems, where they can lead to program crashes or system instability.

GPL stands for "General Public License" and is a widely used free software license, created by the Free Software Foundation (FSF), that ensures software users have the freedom to use, study, modify, and distribute the software. Under the terms, users are granted the freedom to run the software for any purpose, to study how the software works and adapt it to their needs, to redistribute copies, and to improve and distribute modified versions of the software. However, there are obligations, such as ensuring that the source code of the software and any modifications are also made freely available to others.

GPRS stands for General Packet Radio Service and is an enhancement for GSM and TDMA core networks that introduces packet data transmission. GPRS uses radio spectrum very efficiently and provides users with "always on" connectivity and greater bandwidth.

GPS stands for Global Positioning System and is a satellite-based positioning system that provides a three-dimensional position on the Earth's surface, commonly used navigation systems such as satellite navigation (sat-nav).

GPT stands for GUID Partition Table and is the scheme used to define hard disk partitions on computers with UEFI firmware. GPT replaces MBR.

GPU (Graphics Processing Unit) is a specialized processor designed to accelerate the rendering of images, 3D graphics, and complex visual computations.

Gradient in graphics, is a area with a smooth blend from one colour to another.

Graphic User Interface or Graphical User Interface (GUI), is a system of interactive visual components such as windows, menus and icons used to convey information to the user and represent commands and applications. The user clicks on icons to start apps, and selects commands from menus to execute operations or tasks.

Information is conveyed to the user using dialog boxes or windows. Microsoft Windows, MacOS, iOS, Linux, and Android all use a Graphic User Interfaces.

Graphics Card or video card is responsible for processing video, graphics and visual effects you see on your monitor.

Graphics Library is a programming library that includes a defined set of primitives and function calls that enable the programmer to draw lines and create shapes in a computer program.

Graphics Processor is the specialised processor at the heart of the graphics card. Modern chipsets can also integrate video processing, 3D polygon setup and texturing routines, and, in some cases, the RAMDAC.

Greyscale is shades of grey that represent light and dark portions of an image. Colour images can also be converted to greyscale where the colours are represented by various shades of grey.

GSM (Global System for Mobile Communications) operates on frequency bands including 850 MHz, 900 MHz, 1800 MHz, and 1900 MHz, depending on the region.

GUI see Graphical User Interface

GUID stands for Globally Unique Identifier and is a 128bit identifier used to uniquely identify user accounts in windows, as well as documents, hardware components, and applications.

Guide Rails are the plastic or metal strips attached to the sides of a hard disk drive mounted in an IBM compatible computer so that the drive easily slides into place.

Gzip (GNU zip) is an open-source utility used compress files. Developed as part of the GNU project, Gzip employs the DEFLATE compression algorithm to efficiently compress data, making it ideal for conserving disk space and reducing transmission time over networks. It is commonly used from the command line to compress files into a single archive with the ".gz" extension. Gzip is widely used in software distribution, file archiving, and data compression tasks.

H.264 also known as Advanced Video Coding (AVC) or MPEG-4 part 10 and is a popular video codec for encoding high quality video used in digital broadcast, internet, and video streaming services.

H.265 also known as High Efficiency Video Coding (HEVC) and is the successor to H.264. H.265 offers more efficient compression and enables encoding and streaming of HD, 4K and 8K video.

Half Adder is a combination logic circuit used in the addition of two bits.

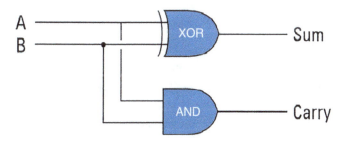

A half adder consists of an eXclusive OR and an AND gate.

A	B	Sum	Carry
0	0	0	0
0	1	1	0
1	0	1	0
1	1	0	1

Half-Duplex is data transmission in both directions, but only in one direction at a time.

Halftone is a method of expressing colour gradation in continuous tone images. The image is resolved into dots, with dark colour being expressed by a large number of dots and diluted colour is by a smaller number of dots. The dot patterns used are called dithers.

Handoff is a continuity feature available on apple devices that allows you to start a task on one device and finish it on another.

Handshake is an automated process of negotiation between two devices preceding a connection.

Hard Disk is a storage medium that stores data as magnetic patterns on a rigid disk, usually made of a magnetic thin film deposited on an aluminium or glass platter. Magnetic read/write heads are mounted on an actuator arm that moves back and forth across the surface of the platter.

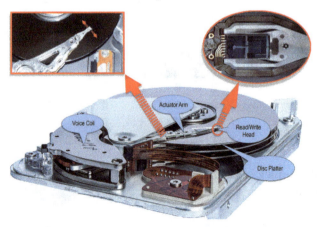

Hard Error is a data error that occurs on a disk and is usually caused by defects in the surface.

Harvard Architecture developed in early computer systems where instructions and data were stored on punch cards or punched paper tape. The photograph below is the Harvard Mark I built by IBM in 1944.

The Mark I read its instructions from a punched paper tape. A separate tape contained data for input. This separation of data and instructions is known as the Harvard architecture.

Here in the diagram below, you can see on the Harvard architecture, there is a separate area for program instructions and another for data.

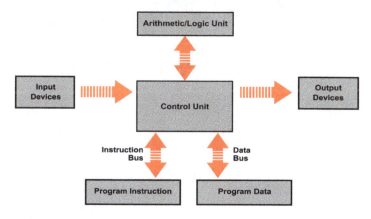

Many embedded systems in use today are based on the Harvard architecture.

143

HDCP stands for High-bandwidth Digital Content Protection and is an encoding method used for distributing digital content via a DP, DVI or HDMI. Using hardware on both the graphics card and the monitor, HDCP encrypts data on route to a display device, where it is then decrypted.

HDLC stands for High-level Data Link Control and is an ISO communications protocol used in X.25 packet switching networks. The HDLC protocol embeds information in a data frame that allows devices to control data flow and correct errors at the data link layer.

HDMI stands for High Definition Media Interface and is an interface for connecting to TVs, monitors, projectors, set top boxes, dvd/bluray players, media streaming devices and so forth. This interface carries both digital audio and video on a single cable. There are three sizes of connectors: standard, mini and micro.

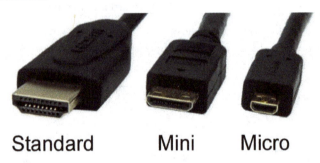

Standard   Mini   Micro

HDTV short for High Definition TV and is a television system with a resolution greater than 525- line and 625-line systems and a picture aspect ratio of 16:9. Common HDTV formats:

720p (1280x720) with 921,600 pixels.

1080i (1920×1080) interlaced scan with 2,073,600 pixels.

1080p (1920×1080) progressive scan with 2,073,600 pixels:

Head is the tiny electromagnetic coil used to read and write magnetic data patterns on a disk.

Head Crash is damage to a read / write head on a magnetic disk, caused when the head hit the disk surface. A head crash can also be caused by dust and other contamination inside the drive enclosure.

Heat Sink is a metallic structure attached to a semiconductor device such as a CPU, that dissipates the heat to the surrounding environment.

HEVC or H.265, is short for High Efficiency Video Coding and is a video compression standard that offers better compression to H.264. See H.265.

Hexadecimal also known as base 16, and is a numbering system of 16 digits often used as a short hand for binary notation. Hexadecimal uses the numbers 0-9, and the letters A-F:

Hex	0	1	2	3	4	5	6	7	8	9	A	B	C	D	E	F
Dec	0	1	2	3	4	5	6	7	8	9	10	11	12	13	14	15

Hierarchical Database is a database where the data is organized into a tree-like structure with a single parent for each record

High Colour is any graphics that are 16-bit and contain up to 65,536 colours.

High-Level Formatting is disk format operation performed by the operating system's format program such as the format command in Linux or Windows 10. Among other things, the formatting program creates the root directory, file allocation tables, and other basic configurations. See also Low-Level Formatting.

High-Level Language is a computer programming language that allows a programmer to write programs in a more human-like language that focuses on logic rather than a particular type of computer hardware. Code is then either compiled or interpreted for execution. Examples include C, C++, Python, and Java

Highlights are the bright parts of an image (eg the sky).

Histogram is a graphical representation of the tonal distribution in a digital image. The sky is represented by the highlights and whites as these are the brightest tones. In contrast the darkest parts of the image are represented by the blacks and shadows.

Home Theatre system is a audio visual system combining components such as live TV, DVD and video streaming at home in order to recreate the experience of watching a movie in the cinema.

Host is any device connected to a TCP/IP network such as the internet, that has a live IP address.

Host Adapter is a circuit board or card that plugs into a slot on the motherboard and acts as the interface between the system bus and a peripheral device.

Hot Swap is the removal or addition of components to a computer system without first shutting down. With a hot swapping, you can add a hard disk or remove it while the computer system is running.

Hostname is a unique name for a device on a network that is used to identify the device in electronic communication.

HPM short for Hyper Page Mode, in DRAM operation, another term for EDO or Extended Data Out.

HRTF stands for Head-Related Transfer Functions and refers to the mathematics that models the way a human ear localises the direction of a sound.

HSB short for Hue Saturation Brightness, a way of describing colour in a more human friendly way. With the HSB model, all colours can be defined by expressing their levels of hue as a number of degrees on the colour wheel.

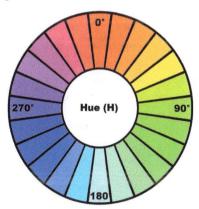

Saturation and brightness are expressed as a percentage. The saturation is the intensity of the hue.

Here in Photoshop's colour picker we can see the HSB values for the selected colour.

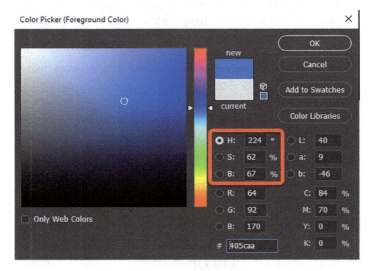

HSCSD stands for High Speed Circuit Switched Data and is the final evolution of circuit switched data within the GSM environment. HSCSD enables the transmission of data over a GSM link at speeds of up to 57.6kbit/s. This is achieved by concatenating consecutive GSM timeslots, each of which is capable of supporting 14.4kbit/s. Up to four GSM timeslots are needed for the transmission of HSCSD.

HSF stands for Horizontal Scanning Frequency and indicates the speed, measured in kilohertz, at which a single horizontal line is drawn on the screen. Higher scan rates are needed to provide sharper, crisper images at higher resolutions. Also called scan rate.

HTML stands for Hypertext Markup Language and is an ASCII text-based, script- like language used for creating hypertext documents for the World Wide Web.

HTML5 is the fifth and current major version of the HTML standard. It is a markup language used for structuring and presenting content on the World Wide Web.

HTPS stands for High Temperature Poly-Silicon and is a thin-film transistor (TFT) panel is an active matrix display containing a microscopic thin-film transistor in the corner of each pixel. HTPS panels allow driver ICs to be embedded into their TFTs, thereby allowing greater miniaturisation (higher pixel counts and higher aperture ratios).

HTTP stands for Hypertext Transfer Protocol and is the way a web browser and the server communicate to deliver web pages.
`http://www.elluminetpress.com`

HTTPS stands for Hypertext Transfer Protocol Secure and is the way a web browser and web server communicate to deliver web pages. The protocol builds on HTTP by adding a secure encrypted connection between server and host using Transport Layer Security (TLS) or Secure Sockets Layer (SSL).

For example: `https://www.elluminetpress.com`

HTTP/2 is the second major version of the Hypertext Transfer Protocol, used by the World Wide Web. It was developed by the HTTP Working Group of the Internet Engineering Task Force (IETF) and published as an IETF standard in May 2015. HTTP/2 focuses on performance improvements over HTTP/1.1 by enabling a more efficient use of network resources and a reduced perception of latency. It introduces several key enhancements such as binary framing, multiplexing (allowing multiple requests and responses to be in flight at the same time on the same connection), header compression to reduce overhead, and server push capabilities. These features make websites load faster without requiring changes to existing applications.

HTTP/3 is the third major version of the Hypertext Transfer Protocol (HTTP), designed to improve web performance by reducing latency and packet loss. It is based on the QUIC transport protocol, originally developed by Google. QUIC provides a foundation for HTTP/3 to improve upon the performance issues related to HTTP/2, especially in the context of lossy networks where packet loss can significantly degrade performance. HTTP/3 further reduces latency by employing QUIC's ability to establish connections more quickly, handle packet loss better, and support multiplexed streams over a single connection without head-of-line blocking issues found in TCP-based HTTP/2. It was developed to enhance web performance and security.

Hub is more or less obsolete nowadays. A hub was a common connection point for devices in a network, often used at the centre of a star-topology network. A hub is a multiport repeater, a packet entering a port on the hub is broadcast to every other port. Network switches have largely replaced hubs on ethernet networks.

Hue is another word for colour often used as a term for the pure spectrum colours such as red, orange, yellow, blue, green, and violet.

Huffman Coding is a lossless data compression algorithm based on the frequency of occurrence of a data item. Codes of different lengths are assigned to characters based on the frequency of occurrence. Smaller codes are assigned to characters that have the highest occurrence.

For example encoding the string LEMMONS, E would be encoded as 101, whereas M would be encoded as 01 as it appears more often.

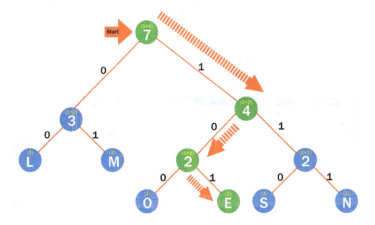

HVD stands for High Voltage Differential and is the logic signalling system originally defined in the SCSI-2 standard. HVD has a maximum logic voltage of 5V and uses a paired plus and minus signal level to reduce the effects of noise on the SCSI bus. It was functionally replaced by LVD (Low Voltage Differential) in the SCSI-3 variant of the standard. HVD and LVD SCSI are not directly compatible but can be interconnected by the use of a special adapter.

Hyperlink is a pointer from text or an image map to a page or other type of file on the world wide web. On web pages, hyperlinks are the primary way to navigate between pages and among web sites.

Hyperthreading is Intel's hardware technology that allows more than one thread to run on each CPU core. Each physical core on the CPU is split into virtual cores called threads and appear as separate physical CPUs to the operating system

HyperTransport is an industry standard high-speed, high-performance, point-to-point connection method for integrated circuits pioneered by AMD. It initially allowed for connection speeds of up to 6.4GBps.

Hyper-V is a virtualization software developed by Microsoft that allows for the creation and management of virtual machines on Windows-based systems. It enables users to run multiple operating systems on a single physical server, essentially partitioning it into multiple distinct servers.

Hypervisor is a piece of software, firmware, or hardware that creates and runs virtual machines (VMs). A hypervisor allows one host computer to support multiple guest VMs by virtually sharing its resources, such as memory and processing power. There are two types of hypervisors: Type 1 (or bare-metal hypervisors) run directly on the host's hardware to control the hardware and manage guest operating systems. Examples include VMware ESXi, Microsoft Hyper-V, and Xen. Type 2 (or hosted hypervisors) run on a conventional operating system just like other computer programs. Examples include VMware Workstation and Oracle VirtualBox. Hypervisors are crucial in cloud computing environments, allowing for efficient resource utilization, isolation, and scalability.

Hz (Hertz) is unit of frequency in the International System of Units (SI) that measures the number of cycles per second of a periodic phenomenon. Named after the German physicist Heinrich Hertz, one hertz (1 Hz) equals one cycle per second. The hertz is commonly used to specify the frequencies of anything that oscillates, such as sound waves, radio waves, and the clock speeds of computers.

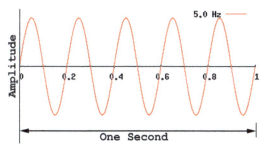

For example, the standard pitch reference for music tuning, the note A above middle C, is typically defined as 440 Hz, meaning the sound wave of this note oscillates 440 times per second. In computing, processors are often rated in gigahertz (GHz), where one GHz represents one billion cycles per second, indicating the speed at which a computer's CPU can process instructions.

I

I/O stands for Input/Output and refers to data transfer from input devices such as a keyboard, mouse, or scanner, to and output device such as a printer or monitor.

I/O Address is the memory location for a particular device (disk drive, sound card, printer port, etc.). Two devices cannot share the same I/O address space.

IA-32 stands for Intel Architecture 32-bit. Intel's 32-bit architecture, also known as x86. IA-32 chips span the early 1990s Intel 486 series to the seventh-generation Intel Pentium 4 and AMD Athlon chips. See also IA-64.

IA-64 stands for Intel Architecture 64-bit and is a 64-bit architecture jointly developed by HP and Intel with IA-32 compatibility. IA-64 supports 32-bit and 64- bit environments, and provides compatibility with IA-32 systems.

IBM PC (model 5150) launched in 1981, using an Intel 8088 processor. The IBM PC AT (5170), introduced in 1984, was an advanced model featuring an Intel 80286 running at 6–8 MHz, 256K RAM, and MS-DOS 3.0.

IANA (Internet Assigned Numbers Authority) is responsible for the technical maintenance of the assignments of unique identifiers for internet protocols, IP address space allocation, and the management of the DNS root zone. This function includes oversight of the global IP address allocation, management of the DNS root, and coordination of the system that ensures each domain name maps to the correct IP address. Originally operated by the University of Southern California under contract with the U.S. Department of Defense, the IANA functions were transitioned to ICANN in 1998.

IC stands for Integrated Circuit and is a small electronic component produced in or on a small slice of silicon called a wafer. Its name comes from the integration of transistors, resistors and capacitors on a single chip.

ICANN (Internet Corporation for Assigned Names and Numbers) is a nonprofit organization responsible for coordinating the maintenance and procedures of several databases related to the namespaces and numerical spaces of the Internet, ensuring the network's stable and secure operation. ICANN's functions include overseeing the distribution of unique IP addresses and domain names (overseeing the DNS root, managing the domain name system's top-level development, and policy-making), as well as the accreditation of domain name registrars.

IDE is short for Integrated Device Electronics or Intelligent Drive Electronics and is a drive-interface specification for disk drives in which all the drive's control electronics are part of the drive itself, rather than on a separate adapter connecting the drive to the expansion bus. See EIDE and SCSI.

IDE is Short for Integrated Development Environment and is a software development tool containing a source code editor, compiler, and debugger.

IEEE stands for Institute of Electrical and Electronics Engineers and is a membership organisation that includes engineers, scientists and students in electronics and allied fields. The IEEE sets standards for computers and communications, such as IEEE 802 standards for Local Area Networks, 802.3 for ethernet, 802.11 for WiFi and 1394 for firewire.

iMac is an all in one computer developed by Apple intended for use at home, in schools, and small offices, and promoted as an easy-to-use, stylish computer

Image is a computerised representation of a picture or graphic.

Image Resolution is the fineness or coarseness of an image as it was digitised, measured in Dots Per Inch (DPI), typically from 72 to 400 DPI.

IMAP stands for Internet Message Access Protocol, an email protocol that allows you to directly manage your emails on the email server without having to download them to a mail client program first.

IMT-2000 stands for International Mobile Telecommunications 2000 and is a worldwide set of standards for the 3rd generation cellular communications.

Index is a pointer used to indicate a specific location.

Inheritance in computer programming is the feature of an object class to take on characteristics of its parent.

Here we have a parent class called Person, and two child classes called Student and Staff. The child classes inherit all the attributes and methods of the parent classes. Child classes can

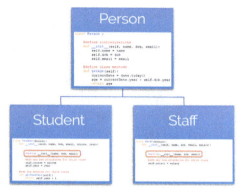

include any additional attributes and methods that are not accessible from other classes.

Inkjet is a printer technology where ink is fired onto the printer paper to form an image or character.

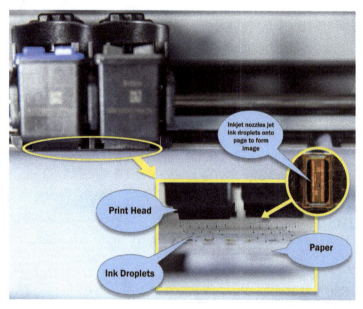

Instruction Cache is a temporary store of instructions usually on CPU allowing quick access.

Instruction Set is the complete set of instructions that can be executed by a processor.

Interactive Video is the combination of video and a computer program running under the control of the user where the viewer's decisions affect the way in which the video unfolds.

Integer is a whole number that can be either positive, negative, or zero, without any fractional or decimal parts.

Interface is a shared link in which two or more separate components of a computer system can communicate and exchange information such as the various buses, storage devices such as IDE, SATA, SCSI, and other I/O devices.

Interframe Coding is a compression techniques that encodes the differences between frames of video.

Interlaced is a scheme used to render a video image by displaying alternate scan lines in two discrete fields.

First Scan   Second Scan

Interleave refers to the arrangement of sequential data in a non sequential way to increase performance.

Interleave Factor is a technique used by older hard disk drives to arrange sectors in a non-contiguous way so as to reduce latency thereby increasing read/write performance. The interleave factor specifies the physical spacing between consecutive logical sectors.

Internal Drive is a drive mounted inside one of a computer's drive bays (or a hard disk on a card, which is installed in one of the computer's slots).

InterNIC is a term historically associated with the Internet Network Information Center, an organization that played a pivotal role in the administration and registration of domain names and IP addresses on the Internet. Established in the early 1990s, InterNIC was responsible for providing central Internet registry services which included the allocation of IP addresses and the management of the DNS (Domain Name System). Over time, as the Internet grew and evolved, the functions of InterNIC were transitioned to various other organizations, most notably to the Internet Corporation for Assigned Names and Numbers (ICANN) in 1998, which now oversees the global DNS, IP address allocation, and other critical Internet infrastructure services. InterNIC was foundational in establishing the structured administration of Internet resources

Internet refers to the vast global network of interconnected computers, networks and devices that communicate with each other using a standardized communication protocol such as Transmission Control Protocol/Internet Protocol (TCP/IP). It is a network of networks that consists of private, public, academic, business, and government networks of local to global scope, linked by a broad array of electronic, wireless, and optical networking technologies. Originating from ARPANET, a research network developed by the United States Department of Defense in the late 1960s, the Internet has evolved to become the principal infrastructure for global communication, information exchange, and commerce. It supports an extensive range of activities, including social networking, online gaming, data transfer, digital media streaming, e-commerce and the world wide web, making it an essential element of modern life.

Internet of Things (IoT) refers to the network of physical objects—devices, vehicles, appliances, and other items embedded with sensors, software, and other technologies— aimed at connecting and exchanging data with other devices and systems over the internet. These objects, often called "smart" devices, can collect, transmit, and act on data, often with minimal human intervention. The IoT merges the digital and physical worlds, opening up a wide range of possibilities for smart homes, smart cities, industrial automation, healthcare, and beyond. It allows for more directly integrated computer-based systems into the physical environment, enhancing efficiency, economic benefits, and reducing human exertions. IoT systems can range from simple environmental monitoring to complex industrial machinery that uses sophisticated software and hardware to manage and process data, all connected through a global network.

Intranet is usually a private network designed to share information, collaboration and various other computing services within an organisation

Interpreter is a translator that converts one high level language program statement into machine code at a time and then executes it, before moving onto the next statement. Python and Javascript are interpreted programming language.

Invar is a type of metal used in the shadow mask that provides more consistent images over time, by reducing warping of the shadow mask when bright images are displayed.

Inverse Kinematics is process of calculating the variable parameters needed to determine the motion of a robot or animated character to reach a position relative to the start. For example when building a robotic arm to perform a task, inverse kinematics can determine an appropriate joint configuration to move the arm to a specific position.

Ion is an atom or molecule that has a net electrical charge. A positive ion is called a cation (pronounced "cat-eye-on") as it has fewer electrons than protons, and a negative ion is called an anion (pronounced "an-eye-on") as it has more electrons than protons. In semiconductor manufacturing, ions are the source of chemical impurities that alter the conductivity of silicon.

iOS is a mobile operating system developed by Apple for their line of iPads and iPhones.

IP Address stands for Internet Protocol, a numerical address assigned to each device connected to a computer network. IPv4 defines an IP address as a 32-bit number divided into four 8 bit octets, and is usually expressed as a dotted decimal number each ranging from 1 to 254. Eg 192.168.1.2. IPv6 uses eight 16-bit hexadecimal numbers separated by a colon. Eg: fdaa:bbcc:ddee:0000:71a4:c9d5:57d4:ec99

IPC stands for Instructions Per Clock and is a measure of how many instructions a CPU is capable of executing in a single clock. Since different processor architectures have different

IPv4 stands for Internet Protocol Version 4. A numerical address assigned to each device connected to a computer network. IPv4 defines an IP address as a 32-bit number divided into four 8 bit octets, and is usually expressed as a dotted decimal number each ranging from 1 to 254. Eg:

192.168.1.2

IPv6 stands for Internet Protocol Version 6, a numerical address assigned to each device connected to a computer network. IPv6 uses eight 16-bit hexadecimal numbers separated by a colon. Eg:

An IPv6 address can be broken down into various parts to identify the site or organisation, network, and device.

IRQ stands for Interrupt ReQuest and is a signal generated by a device to request processing time from the CPU. Each time a keyboard button is pressed or a character is printed to a screen, an IRQ is generated by the requesting device. IRQ signals are transmitted along IRQ lines which connect peripheral devices to a programmable interrupt controller, or PIC.

ISA stands for Industry Standard Architecture and is the architectural standard for the IBM XT (8-bit) and the IBM AT (16-bit) bus designs. In ISA systems, an adapter added by plugging the card into one of the 16-bit expansion slots enables expansion devices like network cards, video adapters and modems to send data to and receive data from the PC's CPU and memory 16 bits at a time. See also EISA.

ISDN stands for Integrated Services Digital Network and is the CCITT standard that defines a completely digital telephone/telecommunications network which carries voice, data, and video over existing telephone network infrastructure. ISDN provides two 64 Kbit/s channels, which can be combined or used independently for both voice and data. It is designed to provide a single interface for hooking up a phone, fax machine, PC, etc.

ISO stands for International Standards Organisation and is an international body responsible for establishing and managing various standards committees and expert groups, including several image-compression standards.

ISO Image is an archive file that contains an exact replica or copy of the contents of an optical disc, such as a CD, DVD, or Blu-ray. This image format is named after the International Organization for Standardization (ISO), which standardized the format for these disc images. ISO images are commonly used for distributing software, operating systems, and other data that would traditionally be stored on a physical disc. They allow for easy replication and distribution of the contents of a disc, often used for installation or backup purposes. You can mount the ISO image as a virtual disk on your computer. This virtual disk behaves like a physical optical drive, allowing you to access the files and folders contained on the ISO image as if it were inserted into a physical drive. You can also 'burn' the ISO image to a flash drive which is often used as a bootable drive for installing operating systems onto a blank computer.

Isochronous refers to processes where data must be delivered within certain time constraints. For example, multimedia streams require an isochronous transport mechanism to ensure that data is delivered as fast as it is displayed and to ensure that the audio is synchronised with the video. See Asynchronous and Synchronous.

ISP (Internet Service Provider) is an organization that provides services for accessing the Internet. ISPs can be commercial, non-profit, privately owned, or community-owned companies that offer a range of internet-related services, including web access, domain name registration, hosting, and email services. ISPs connect customers to the internet by various means, including DSL (Digital Subscriber Line), cable modem, wireless or dedicated high-speed interconnects. They play a critical role in the internet ecosystem by enabling users to connect to the world wide web, engage in online communications, social media, streaming and access other internet-based services. The scope of services offered by ISPs can vary widely, from providing basic internet access to homes and businesses, to offering comprehensive packages that include web hosting, IT services, and cybersecurity solutions.

ITU stands for International Telecommunications Union and is the United Nations agency for telecommunications. The ITU combines the standards- setting activities of the predecessor organisations formerly called the International Telegraph and Telephone Consultative Committee (CCITT) and the International Radio Consultative Committee (CCIR), being charged with establishing and co-ordinating standards for electronic communications worldwide.

iTunes is a now deprecated media player app developed by Apple that allowed users to purchase and download music. iTunes was later split into the music app, podcasts app and the TV app.

J

Jack is a physical interface for plugging in a corresponding plug or jack plug to establish a connection. Eg, 3.5mm audio jack.

Jaggies also known as Aliasing. A term for the jagged visual appearance of lines and shapes in raster pictures that results from producing graphics on a grid format.

JAR (Java ARchive) file is a compressed file format used for aggregating multiple Java class files, associated resources, and metadata into a single archive. It is a standard way of packaging Java applications and libraries for distribution and deployment. JAR files are similar to ZIP files but specifically designed for Java applications, providing features such as compression, manifest files for metadata, and support for executable JARs. They are widely used in Java development for bundling libraries, frameworks, and executable applications in a portable and efficient manner.

Java is an object oriented programming language originally developed by Sun Microsystems and used in embedded devices, mobile phones, supercomputers and web applications on the internet.

JavaScript is a dynamic programming language commonly used in web development to create interactive effects within web browsers. As an integral part of web applications, it allows developers to implement complex features on web pages—everything from updating content, and controlling multimedia, to animating images, and much more. Initially only used on the client-side, JavaScript has become increasingly prevalent on the server-side as well with the advent of platforms like Node.js.

JEDEC is an organisation that establishes standards for memory operation, features, and packaging.

Jitter refers to the variation in signal timing, often leading to distortion in digital communication, video playback, and networking. In display screens, jitter can cause visual distortions when clock and phase settings are misaligned. In networking, jitter affects data transmission, causing packet delays and affecting real-time applications like VoIP and video streaming.

Joliet is a Microsoft-developed extension to the ISO 9660 file system used on CD-ROMs. It allows long file names (up to 64 characters) and supports Unicode characters, improving compatibility for multilingual file names on Windows systems.

JPEG short for Joint Photographic Experts Group, is a lossy image compression format that uses the Discrete Cosine Transform (DCT) algorithm to reduce image file size while balancing quality. It is widely used for digital photography and web images, offering adjustable compression levels to control image quality.

High Compression

Low Compression

JPEG 2000 is an image compression standard and file format developed by the Joint Photographic Experts Group (JPEG). It provides an efficient method for compressing and storing images while maintaining high quality. Unlike traditional JPEG compression, which is based on the discrete cosine transform (DCT), JPEG 2000 uses wavelet-based compression techniques. This allows for better preservation of image details and reduces artifacts such as blocking and ringing.

JRE stands for Java Runtime Environment, is a software package that provides the necessary runtime components for executing Java applications. It includes the Java Virtual Machine (JVM), libraries, and other supporting files required for running Java programs. The JRE allows users to run Java applications on their machines without needing to develop or compile Java code themselves. It provides a platform-independent environment, enabling Java programs to run consistently across different operating systems and hardware architectures. The JRE also includes tools such as the Java Control Panel and Java Web Start, which facilitate the deployment and management of Java applications.

JSON (JavaScript Object Notation) a lightweight data interchange format that is easy for humans to read and write, and easy for machines to parse and generate. It is based on a subset of the JavaScript programming language and serves as a format for transmitting structured data over a network connection. JSON is commonly used for representing and exchanging data between a server and a web application, but it is also widely used in other contexts due to its simplicity and flexibility. JSON data is organized into key-value pairs and supports various data types such as strings, numbers, arrays, and objects. It has become a standard for data interchange on the web due to its simplicity, readability, and widespread support across programming languages and platforms. For example.

```
{
  "name": "Alice",
  "age": 25,
  "city": "Seattle"
}
```

"name", "age", and "city" are keys.

"Alice", 25, and "Seattle" are the corresponding values, representing a person's name, age, and city.

Jumper is a small metal block with plastic covered handles for enabling or disabling specific functions on a motherboard or expansion card.

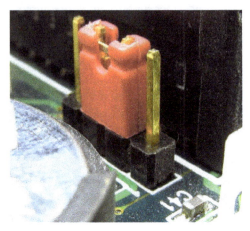

Just-Noticeable Difference In the CIELAB colour model, a difference in hue, chroma, or intensity, or some combination of all three, that is apparent to a trained observer under ideal lighting conditions. A just-noticeable difference is a change of 1; a change of 5 is apparent to most people most of the time.

JVM stands for Java Virtual Machine, is a crucial component of the Java Runtime Environment (JRE) responsible for executing Java bytecode. It acts as an abstract computing machine, providing a runtime environment for Java applications to run on various hardware and operating systems without modification. The JVM interprets compiled Java bytecode or just-in-time (JIT) compiles it into native machine code for execution by the underlying hardware. It manages memory allocation and garbage collection, facilitates dynamic class loading, and ensures platform independence by abstracting hardware-specific functionalities. The JVM also provides various tools for monitoring, profiling, and debugging Java applications, contributing to Java's robustness and portability across different environments.

170

K

K56flex is a protocol jointly developed by Lucent Technologies and Rockwell International Corp to achieve 56 Kbit/s modem transmissions over ordinary phone lines. K56flex allows downloads at up to 56 Kbit/s; uploads are limited to the normal V.34 speed of 33.6 Kbit/s. See also X2.

Kali Linux is a specialized Linux distribution designed for cybersecurity professionals, ethical hackers, and penetration testers. It is developed and maintained by Offensive Security. Kali Linux comes pre-installed with numerous tools and utilities used for various cybersecurity tasks, including penetration testing, digital forensics, reverse engineering, and security research. Kali Linux is widely used in the cybersecurity industry for assessing and securing networks, systems, and applications.

KB stands for Kilobyte, a unit of data storage equivalent to 1000 bytes. A Kibibyte is 1024 bytes. See KiB.

Kbit is short for Kilobit and is a unit of measure consisting of 1000 bits. The unit often used in expressions of data transmission capacity.

Kbit/s is short for Kilobits Per Second (or Kbps) and is a measure of data transfer speed. Note that 1 Kbit/s is 1,000 bits per second. Data transfer rates are measured using the decimal meaning of K whereas data storage is measured using the powers-of-2 meaning of K.

Kbps short for Kilobits per second. Note lowercase 'b'.

KBps short for Kilobytes per second, a performance measure used for mass storage devices and memory systems. Note uppercase 'B'.

Kerberos is a network authentication protocol designed to provide secure authentication for client-server applications. It primarily uses symmetric cryptography but also incorporates asymmetric cryptography during the initial key exchange. It employs a ticket-based system, where a trusted Key Distribution Center (KDC) issues encrypted tickets for mutual authentication.

Kernel is the core component of an operating system that manages system resources, including memory, processes, and hardware communication. It provides a bridge between software and hardware through system calls. Examples include the Linux kernel and the Windows NT kernel.

Kerning is the process of adjusting the spacing between two individual font characters.

Kerr Effect is a change in rotation of light reflected off a magnetic field. The polarity of a magneto-optic bit causes the laser to shift one degree clockwise or counter clockwise.

Keyboard is an input device primarily used to enter characters such as letters, numbers and symbols into a computer, as well as to execute various functions by pressing shortcut or function keys. Along the top you'll often find function keys and an alphanumeric QWERTY keyboard. To the right you'll find various command keys such as insert, delete, etc, along with arrow keys. Some keyboards will also include a numeric keypad on the far right.

Keyframe is a designated frame in animation or a video editing that defines a specific position, state, or effect. The computer automatically generates intermediate frames (tweening) to create smooth transitions between keyframes. In video compression, a keyframe stores a full image, while subsequent frames (called delta frames) only store changes from previous frames.

Keylogger, short for "keystroke logger," is a type of software or hardware device designed to covertly record and monitor the keystrokes typed by a user on a computer keyboard. This information can include passwords, usernames, credit card numbers, and other sensitive data entered by the user. Keyloggers can be used for various purposes, including legitimate ones such as monitoring employee activity or parental control, as well as malicious ones like stealing confidential information for identity theft or unauthorized access to accounts.

Keys are notches carved into the contact edge of a memory module (DRAM DIMM) that prevent them from being plugged into an incompatible system. Also a button on a computer keyboard.

Keystone Distortion is a type of geometric distortion where an image appears trapezoidal instead of rectangular, usually caused by projecting onto a surface at an angle. It can result in inward or outward slanting edges, and is commonly corrected using keystone correction in projectors.

Keyword is a word often used in digital marketing that best describes the content on a page or post. In other words keywords are used by search engines to work out what a page is about. See SEO.

KHz is short for KiloHertz and is a measure of frequency equal to 1000 hertz. See Hz.

KiB stands for Kibibyte and is a unit of measure consisting of 1024 bytes. See also MiB, GiB and TiB.

Kilobyte (KB) derived from the Standards Insitute prefix kilo meaning 1000, a unit of information or computer storage. Abbreviations for kilobyte include KB, kB, Kbyte, and kbyte.

Kiosk Mode refers to a feature or configuration in software or devices that limits the functionality and access of users to a specific set of applications or content. It is commonly used in public settings, such as retail stores, museums, libraries, or airports, where users interact with self-service terminals or interactive displays. In Kiosk Mode, the device or software is typically locked down to prevent users from accessing the underlying operating system or making unauthorized changes, ensuring a controlled and secure user experience.

KMS stands for Key Management Service. It is a technology used by Microsoft to activate and manage product licenses in large-scale environments using a centralized server rather than individual product keys.

Knowledge Base is a large collection of articles and documents maintained by a company as part of their customer support to assist customers with problems.

KVM Switch short for Keyboard, Video, Mouse switch, is a hardware device used to control multiple computers or servers from a single set of peripherals, including a keyboard, monitor, and mouse.

176

L

LAN is a small network contained on a single site or building. As you can see in the diagram below, the network covers a small area. The computers could be split up into different offices or all in one room and can all access resources served from the file server and use internet services provided by the router.

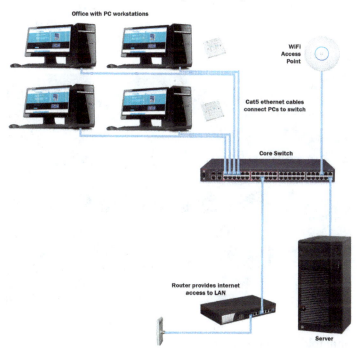

Office with PC workstations

WiFi Access Point

Cat5 ethernet cables connect PCs to switch

Core Switch

Router provides internet access to LAN

Server

All the machines on the network are connected using wired (such as Cat5e, Cat6) or wireless (Wi-Fi) connections through a switch.

Landing Zone is the non-data area set-aside on a hard drive platter for the heads to rest when the system powers down.

LAPM stands for Link Access Procedure For Modems and is one of the two protocols specified by V.42. LAPM provides error control when a modem is communicating with another modem that supports LAPM.

Laser Disc is an obsolete optical disk that was used for full-motion video. In the 1970s, various videodisc systems were introduced, but only the Philips LaserVision survived.

Laser Printer is a type of printer that utilises a laser beam to produce an image on a drum. The light of the laser alters the electrical charge on the drum wherever it hits. The drum is then rolled through a reservoir of toner, which is picked up by the charged portions

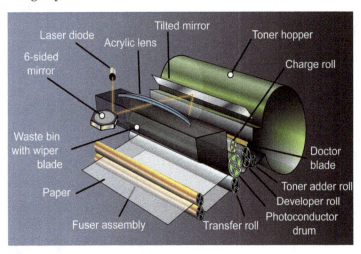

Latch is a circuit element that stores a given value on its output until told to store a different value.

Latency is the time between initiating a request for data and the beginning of the actual data transfer. For example, the average latency of a hard disk drive is easily calculated from the spindle speed, as the time for half a rotation. In communications, network latency is the delay introduced when a packet is momentarily stored, analysed and then forwarded.

Lathing is creating a 3-D surface by rotating a 2-D spline around an axis.

LBA is short for Logical Block Addressing and is the scheme by which the BIOS passes an operating system request for a given sector to a modern hard drive.

LCD stands for Liquid Crystal Display and is a display technology that uses polarising light filters and liquid crystal cells to produce an on a screen.

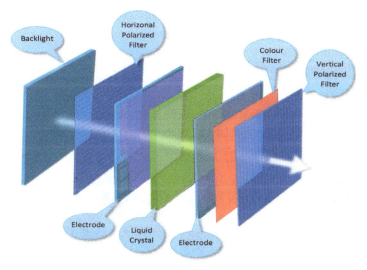

LCD Printer is similar to a laser printer but instead of using a laser to create an image on the drum, the printer shines a light through an LCD panel. Individual pixels in the panel either let the light pass or block it to create the image on the print drum.

LCOS stands for Liquid Crystal on Silicon and is a liquid crystal layer on top of a pixelated, highly-reflective substrate. Below the substrate is a backplane that includes the electronics to drive the pixels. The backplane and liquid crystals are combined into a panel and packaged for use in a projection subsystem or "light engine."

LDAP or Lightweight Directory Access Protocol, is a protocol used for accessing and managing directory information services. It provides a standardized method for querying and modifying directory services, such as user authentication, address book information, and network resources, in a distributed computing environment. LDAP is commonly used in enterprise environments for centralized authentication, directory services, and user management.

LEDs are semiconductor devices that emit light when an electric current passes through them. They come in various colors, and remain widely used  in modern lighting, and backlighting for LCD screens.

LED Printer is an electro-photographic printer similar to a laser printer except it uses a matrix of LEDs as its light source instead of a laser. The LED matrix bar pulse-flashes across the width of the page to create an image on the print drum.

Legacy refers to an application, architecture, protocol, or system that is outdated but still in use. Legacy systems may be difficult to maintain or integrate with modern technologies, yet they remain in operation due to cost, compatibility, or critical business functions.

LEP stands for Light-Emitting Polymer and is a display technology in which plastics are made to conduct electricity and, under certain conditions, emit light.

Level 1 Cache (L1 Cache) is integrated directly into the processor core and operates at the speed of the processor itself, making it the fastest form of cache. It is used to store a small but critical subset of data and instructions that are immediately necessary for the CPU's current operations. Also known as primary or internal cache, L1 cache is typically small, ranging from a few kilobytes to several tens of kilobytes per core.

Level 2 Cache (L2 Cache) is located on the processor chip, close to the CPU cores, but is usually larger than L1 cache. While it is slower than L1 cache, L2 cache still operates at a high speed and serves as a bridge between the ultra-fast L1 cache and the larger but slower L3 cache. It can be dedicated to a single core or shared between a few cores, depending on the processor's architecture. L2 cache is also referred to as secondary cache.

Level 3 Cache (L3 Cache) is typically shared across all cores on the processor and is larger than both L1 and L2 caches. Although it is the slowest among the three levels of cache, L3 cache is still significantly faster than main system memory (RAM). Its primary role is to reduce the average time to access memory by serving as a buffer for the data most frequently accessed by the CPU cores. Because it is shared, L3 cache helps in reducing redundancy among the cache levels and improves efficiency in data retrieval across cores. It is sometimes located on the processor chip, but due to its larger size compared to L1 and L2 caches, it can also be found on a separate die within the CPU package, making the original description of it being "outside the processor core" somewhat misleading in modern processors.

LIFO stands for Last In First Out and is a queuing method in which the next item to be retrieved is the item most recently placed in the queue. See also FIFO.

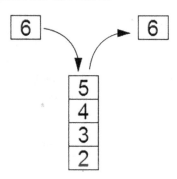

Lighting is an effect in 3D graphics used to simulate light in a scene.

Line Art is a type of graphic consisting entirely of lines, without any shading.

Line Noise is a random signal disturbance that sometimes occurs over a telephone line. Noise can disrupt communications and corrupt the transmitted data. The ratio of the usable signal to unusable noise on a communications link is referred to as the signal-to-noise ratio. Fibre optic cables are far less susceptible to noise than metal wire cables.

Linux is a free and open-source operating system kernel, originally developed by Linus Torvalds. It follows Unix-like principles and serves as the foundation for various Linux distributions (such as Ubuntu, Fedora, and CentOS). Linux is widely used in servers, desktops, mobile devices, and embedded systems

Local Bus is a high-speed data connection between the CPU and main memory, designed to reduce latency and increase performance. Older implementations included VESA Local Bus, while modern systems integrate high-speed interconnects directly into the processor chipset. PCI-Express (PCIe) is a separate high-speed expansion bus used for peripherals like graphics cards and storage devices.

Local Loop are the lines between a customer and the telephone company's central office, often called the last mile. Local loops often use copper cables.

Localhost is the address used to point to the local computer on a network. The IP address is 127.0.0.1, also known as a loopback address.

Logic Gate is an electronic device made up of transistors that implement Boolean logic operations on a circuit board. Transistors make up logic gates which make up circuits, and circuits make up electronic systems.

Here below we have AND, NOT, OR, NAND, NOR, XOR gates.

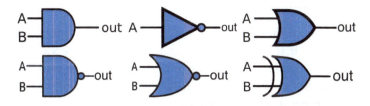

Logical Shift in binary is a shift of the bits to the left or right. A logical shift does not preserve the sign bit (MSB) and is often used when the data is treated as a sequence of bits rather than a number.

Look Ahead is a technique used for buffering data into cache RAM by reading subsequent blocks in advance to anticipate the next request for data. The look ahead technique speeds up disk access of sequential blocks of data.

Loop is a control structure that repeats a block of code multiple times until a specific condition is met. There are various types of loops, including the "for" loop, "while" loop, and "do-while" loop, each with its own syntax and use cases. Loops are commonly used for iterating over arrays, processing lists of data, and implementing repetitive tasks in algorithms and programs.

Loopback Address is 127.0.0.1 or localhost used to identify the local machine on a network. IPv6 loopbacka address is ::1

Loopback Test is a diagnostic test where characters that are sent to the modem are immediately sent back from the modem so the computer can compare the characters sent with the characters received.

Lossless is a compression method for compressing data without losing any information such as GIF or Zip file.

Lossy compression reduces file size by removing some data based on perceptual encoding techniques. This results in smaller files at the cost of some quality loss. Common examples include JPEG for images, MP3 for audio, and H.264 for video.

Low-pass Filter is an electronic circuit or signal processing technique that allows signals with frequencies below a certain cutoff frequency to pass through while attenuating signals with frequencies above the cutoff frequency. It is commonly used in audio processing, telecommunications, and electronic systems to remove high-frequency noise or unwanted signals from a signal while preserving the lower-frequency components.

Low Profile often refers to an expansion card that is designed to fit into a computer case with limited space. These cards have a smaller form factor than standard full-sized cards, making them suitable for  slim or small form factor (SFF) cases often used in business desktops, media centers, and compact personal computers. Low profile cards come with a shorter bracket at the mounting end, which allows them to be installed in the reduced height available in these systems. They maintain the same functionality as their full-sized counterparts but may have some constraints on performance or additional features due to the smaller size and reduced space for components.

Low-Level Formatting is the process often completed by a drive manufacturer to initiate a hard disk drive and prepare it for storing data. The low level format creates tracks and sectors on the surface of the disk. The operating system can then use a high level format to create the file system such as NTFS or FAT32 so users can store data and applications.

LPT1 was the first parallel or printer port on a PC.

LPX is a motherboard form factor which allows for smaller cases used in some desktop model PCs. The distinguishing characteristic of LPX is that expansion boards are inserted into a riser that contains several slots and are therefore parallel, rather than perpendicular, to the motherboard.

LSI stands for Large Scale Integration and refers to the placement of thousands (between 3,000 and 100,000) of electronic components on a single integrated circuit. VLSI (Very Large Scale Integration) is between 100,000 and one million transistors on a chip.

Lumen is a measure of brightness ie the amount of visible light emitted by a light source. Higher the lumen the brighter the light.

Luminance is the amount of light intensity; one of the three image characteristics coded in composite television (represented by the letter Y). May be measured in lux or foot-candles. Also referred to as Intensity.

LZW or Lempel-Ziv-Welch, is a lossless data compression algorithm used to reduce the size of data by encoding repetitive sequences into shorter codes. It was developed by Abraham Lempel, Jacob Ziv, and Terry Welch in the 1980s and is widely used in file compression formats such as GIF (Graphics Interchange Format) and TIFF (Tagged Image File Format). LZW achieves compression by replacing repeated sequences of characters with variable-length codes, resulting in smaller compressed data without loss of information.

M

M.2 is a compact form factor for internal expansion cards, primarily used for SSDs, Wi-Fi adapters, and other peripherals. M.2 supports multiple interfaces, including PCIe, SATA, and USB, allowing for a variety of device application.

The card's connectors are keyed depending on which interface they're compatible with. Here's a summary.

Connector Key	Card Measurements (mm)	Interface	Uses
A	1630, 2230, 3030	PCIe x2, USB 2.0	Wi-Fi and Bluetooth cards
B	2230, 2242, 2260, 2280, 3042, 22110	PCIe x2, SATA, USB 2.0, USB 3.0	SATA and PCIe x2 SSDs
M	2242, 2260, 2280, 22110	PCIe x4, SATA	PCIe x4 SSDs, NVMe

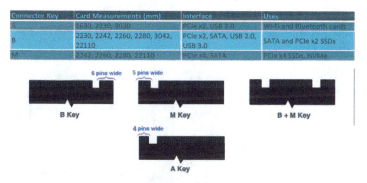

MAC stands for Medium Access Control and is a protocol found on the data link layer of the OSI 7 layer Model, responsible for moving data frames from one Network Interface Card (NIC) to another.

MAC address is a unique identifier assigned to a network interface controller (NIC) for communication on a network. MAC addresses are typically assigned by the manufacturer but can sometimes be changed or spoofed.

Machine Code also known as machine language, is a low-level programming language consisting of binary instructions that can be executed directly by a computer's central processing unit (CPU). Machine code instructions are represented as sequences of binary digits (0s and 1s), corresponding to specific operations such as arithmetic calculations, data manipulation, control flow, and input/output operations.

Machine Learning is a field of artificial intelligence that focuses on the development of computer programs that can access data and use it to learn for themselves. Machine Learning enables computers to recognize patterns and behaviors through algorithms and statistical models, and make decisions with minimal human intervention. Applications of ML range from voice recognition and language translation to complex decision-making systems used in stock trading, autonomous vehicles, and personalized recommendations. The process involves feeding large amounts of data to the algorithm and allowing it to adjust and improve its analytical model through training and testing phases.

Macintosh first introduced by Apple in 1984, marked a breakthrough in personal computer technology, featuring a graphical user interface (GUI) that utilised windows, icons and a mouse for navigation. The success of the Macintosh's GUI led a new age of graphics-based applications and operating systems. Microsoft later  introduced its own GUI-based operating system, Windows, which included some similar design principles.

MacOS is a proprietary graphical operating system developed and marketed by Apple exclusively for the Macintosh line of computers and laptops. Built on a UNIX foundation, macOS incorporates a desktop interface known for its intuitive design and ease of use, featuring elements such as a dock for managing running applications, a finder for file navigation, and a suite of productivity and creative software. Additionally, the Mac App Store offers a vast selection of third-party software, enhancing the versatility and functionality of the platform. Overall, macOS embodies Apple's commitment to delivering a premium computing experience that prioritizes ease of use, reliability, and innovation.

Macro is a predefined sequence of instructions or commands that automates repetitive tasks or complex operations within software applications. These sequences of commands can be recorded or manually programmed, allowing users to execute multiple actions with a single command or keystroke. By automating routine tasks, macros enhance efficiency and productivity, freeing users to focus on more critical aspects of their work. They can be customized to perform specific actions tailored to the user's needs or workflow, making them versatile tools across various software applications such as word processors, spreadsheets, and programming environments. Ultimately, macros streamline workflows, reduce manual labor, and contribute to a smoother user experience in software applications.

Main Memory also known as RAM or primary storage, is the main data storage location where the microprocessor fetches, executes and stores instructions as well as any data required by the instruction.

Malware is short for "malicious software" and refers to any program intentionally designed to cause damage to a computer, server, client, or computer network. This includes a variety of malicious programs such as viruses, worms, Trojan horses, ransomware, spyware, adware, and others. Malware exploits vulnerabilities to compromise system security, steal sensitive data, disrupt operations, and cause harm to the system or its data. It can spread through email attachments, malicious websites, software downloads, and through network connections. Effective countermeasures against malware include the use of antivirus software, firewalls, and other types of security software, as well as practicing safe browsing and email habits.

MAN is short for Metropolitan Area Network. A network spanning a city for example, a university campus.

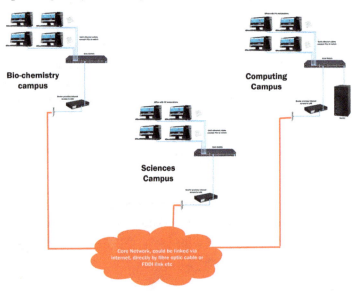

Manual Dialling is dialling a remote modem from a telephone connected to the modem. This is in contrast to automatic dialling, where the modem dials the number.

MAPI is short for Messaging Application Programming Interface and is an API developed by Microsoft and other computer vendors that provides Windows applications with an implementation independent interface to various messaging systems.

Mask are used like stencils in the chip making process. When used with the UV light, masks create the various circuit patterns on each layer of the microprocessor. Also used to describe the information in the alpha channel of a graphic that determines how effects are rendered.

MB stands for Megabyte and is a unit of data storage equivalent to 1 million bytes. 1 Mebibyte (MiB) is 1,048,576 bytes.

Mbit/s is short for Megabits Per Second (or Mbps) and is a measure of data transfer speed. Note that 1 Mbit/s is 1 million bits per second. Data transfer rates are measured using the decimal meaning of M whereas data storage is measured using the powers-of-2 meaning of M.

MBR is short for Master Boot Record, and is the first sector of a disk that identifies where an operating system is located, and how it is booted.

MCA stands for Micro Channel Architecture and is a 32-bit bus architecture introduced by IBM for their PS/2 series microcomputers. Incompatible with original PC/AT (ISA) architecture.

MCI stands for Media Control Interface and is a platform-independent multimedia specification published by Microsoft Corporation and others in 1990 to provide a consistent way to control devices such video playback units.

Media is any component used to store data such as a tape, hard disk, flash drive, DVD, or CD.

Megabyte   derived from the Standards Insitute prefix mega, meaning a million is a unit of computer storage that the equals one million bytes.

Memory Bank is a logical unit of memory in a computer. For example, a 64-bit CPU requires memory banks that provide 64bits of information at a time. A bank can consist of one or more memory modules.

Memory Controller is an essential component that oversees the movement of data into and from main memory.

Memory Cycle is the minimum amount of time required for a memory chip to complete a cycle such as read, write, read/write, or read/modify/write.

Mesh Model is a graphical model with a mesh surface constructed from polygons.

Mesh Network is a network topology in which each node relays data for the network. All nodes cooperate in the distribution of data in the network.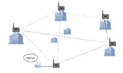

Metadata provides information about other data. It describes the characteristics, origins, usage, and structure of certain data, making it easier to find, use, or manage. Metadata can include titles, descriptions, authorship, creation dates, file sizes, and formats.

Metals such as aluminium and copper are used to conduct the electricity throughout the microprocessor. Gold is also used to connect the actual chip to its package.

Mflops short for Megaflops and is 1 million floating-point instructions per second.

MFM stands for Modified Frequency Modulation and is the data storage system used by floppy disk drives and older early hard disk drives. Had twice the capacity of the earlier FM method but was slower than the competing RLL scheme.

MHz short for Megahertz and is a measurement of frequency in millions of cycles per second.

MiB stands for Mebibyte and is a unit of data storage consisting of 1024KiB or 1,048,576 bytes.

Microcode is the lowest-level instructions that directly control a microprocessor. A single machine-language instruction typically translates into several microcode instructions. In modern PC microprocessors microcode updates can be applied via firmware patches to fix bugs or improve performance.

Microdrive is an ultra-miniature hard disk technology from IBM that uses a single one-inch diameter platter to provide either 170MB or 340MB storage capacity and either one or two GMR heads, the Microdrive is built into a Type II CompactFlash form factor.

Micron μm is a unit of measure equivalent to one-millionth of a metre; synonymous with micrometre.

Microprocessor is an integrated circuit (IC) that serves as the central processing unit (CPU) of a computer or other electronic device. It executes instructions and performs arithmetic and logic operations on data, enabling the device to carry out various tasks and functions.

Microsecond μs is one millionth of a second (.000001 sec.).

Mid Span Repeater is a device that amplifies the signal coming or going to the central office. This device is necessary for ISDN service if you are outside the 18,000 feet distance requirement from the central office.

MIDI stands for Musical Instrument Digital Interface and is a specification that standardises the interface between computers and digital devices that simulate musical instruments. Instead of transmitting large digitised sound samples, the MIDI synthesiser sends commands just a few bytes in length containing information such as instrument, note pitch, duration, volume, attack, and decay. Each channel of a MIDI synthesiser corresponds to a different instrument called a "voice". A MIDI Mapper is a windows multimedia translator for MIDI hardware and software.

Midtones are the parts of an image that are in the middle of the tonal range, halfway between the lightest and the darkest tones.

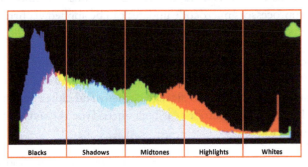

Millisecond One thousandth of a second – 0.001 sec.

MIME stands for Multi-purpose Internet Mail Extension and is the format used for transmitting files across the Internet. Since email messages are designed for text data, this format converts the non text data into a text-based format. Often used for encoding email attachments.

MiniDisc or MD for short is a compact digital audio disc from Sony that comes in read-only and rewritable versions. Introduced in late 1993, the MiniDisc has been popular in Japan. The read-only 2.5in disc stores 140MB compared to 650MB on a CD, but holds the same 74 minutes worth of music  due to Sony's Adaptive Transform Acoustic Coding (ATRAC) compression scheme, which eliminates inaudible portions of the signal.

MiniDVD is a smaller version of the standard DVD disc, MiniDVD (also known as Mini DVD or 8cm DVD) has a diameter of approximately 8 centimeters (3.15  inches), in contrast to the standard DVD size of 12 centimeters (4.72 inches). MiniDVDs are designed to hold smaller amounts of data, typically up to 1.4 GB on a single-sided single-layer disc, which is significantly less than the capacity of standard DVDs.

Minification is the process of removing unnecessary characters and reducing the size of code files, typically in web development, to improve load times and optimize performance. This process involves removing whitespace characters, comments, and other unnecessary formatting from source code files, while preserving the functionality and logic of the code. Minification is commonly applied to HTML, CSS, and JavaScript files used in web development.

Mip Mapping is a sophisticated texturing technique to ensure that 3D objects gain detail smoothly when approaching or receding. This is typically produced in two ways; per-triangle (faster) or per pixel (more accurate).

MIPS stands for Millions of Instructions Per Second and is a measure of the computational performance of a computer's processor, indicating how many million instructions (simple computational tasks) the processor can execute per second. MIPS is used to gauge the speed and efficiency of a processor's execution of its instruction set.

Mirror Site also known as a mirror, is a duplicate or replica website or server that contains identical or nearly identical content to another original website or server. Mirror sites are typically set up for the purpose of distributing content, load balancing, or providing redundancy and backup in case the original site experiences downtime or becomes inaccessible.

Mission Control is a feature native to MacOS that shows every application you have open and allows you to add and manage virtual desktops. You can open mission control by pressing control and the up arrow.

Mixed-Signal Device collects analogue signals and converts them into digital data to be processed. Once a DSP processes and compresses the digital data, a mixed-signal device decompresses, transmits and displays the digital data as either digital or analogue signals.

MMO is Intel's pop-out CPU packaging designed for mobile processors which includes an integrated L2 cache, introduced with Mobile MMX processor launched in early 1998.

MMX stands for MultiMedia eXtensions and was incorporated into Intel's Pentium processor to provide additional instructions designed specifically for processing multimedia data more efficiently. Codenamed P55C.

MNOS stands for Metal Nitride Oxide Semiconductor and is the technology used for EAROMs (Electrically Alterable ROMs); not to be confused with NMOS.

MNP stands for Microcom Networking Protocol and is a series of standards, running from MNP Class 1 to MNP Class 10, designed to improve communications between modems but now superseded by LAPM. They do not stand alone, but operate in conjunction with other modem standards.

Modelling refers to the process of creating a representation of a complex real-world system within a computer or simulation. This representation can be used to analyze, predict, or understand the behavior of the system being modeled. Modelling involves the use of mathematical formulas, algorithms, and data to construct digital simulations or visualizations. These models can be static or dynamic, ranging from simple diagrams to intricate, interactive simulations. In software development and computer science, modelling often involves the use of specific languages or tools, such as UML (Unified Modeling Language) for software architecture, or specialized software for 3D graphics and animation.

Modem is short for MOdulator/DEModulator and is a device that converts digital data into an analogue signal that can be sent across a telephone line (modulation). It also converts the analogue signal it receives from the telephone line, back into digital information (demodulation).

Analog Phone Line

Modes specific frequencies at which the monitor (and/or computer) can display text or graphical information. Most monitors today support several frequencies. This is called multi-frequency or multi-scanning, and it ensures that the monitor will perform with a variety of computers and applications.

Modulation is converting a data stream into analog audio to be sent down a phone line. The opposite is demodulation. See also Modem, PM, FM, AM.

Modulus in programming, is an arithmetic operator that returns the remainder of a division of one number by another.

Moir is a noticeable pattern of interference, often perceived as flickering. For example, a TV image of someone wearing a herringbone jacket can cause the effect. In images of closely spaced lines or other finely detailed patterns, these ripples or waves can appear on colour monitors as well as in scanned images.

Molex is a plastic connector with cylindrical pins often used to supply power to components such as disk drives.

Moore's Law is Gordon Moore's famous prediction that the number of transistors per integrated circuit would double every 18 months..

MOPS stands for Millions of Operations Per Second.

Morph short for metamorphosing, morphing refers to an animation technique in which one image is gradually turned into another.

MOS stands for Metal-Oxide-Semiconductor and are the layers used to create a semiconductor circuit. A thin insulating layer of oxide is deposited on the surface of the wafer. Then a highly conductive layer of tungsten silicide is placed over the top of the oxide dielectric.

Motherboard a large circuit board found in desktop and laptop computer systems that house the majority of the electronics required by the computer such as memory, CPU, as well as various expansions slots and drive interfaces..

Motion Video is video that displays real motion by displaying a sequence of images (called frames) rapidly enough that the eyes see a continuously moving picture.

Motion-JPEG is a video compression format where each frame is compressed individually as a JPEG image, without interframe compression. This results in high-quality but large file sizes..

Mount is to make a file system available for use by a computer's operating system. When a file system is mounted, the operating system can access and interact with the data stored on a storage device, such as a hard drive, SSD, CD-ROM, or network share. The process assigns a mount point to the file system, which is typically a directory within the operating system's file structure. This mount point acts as the root directory for the mounted file system, allowing users and applications to access its contents as if they were part of the local file system hierarchy.

MP stands for Multilink PPP and is a protocol that allows a device to use two PPP communications ports as if they were a single port of greater bandwidth.

MP3 is short for MPEG Audio Layer-3 and is an audio compression format often used to compress music, that employs a lossy compression technique, along with psycho acoustic compression - meaning audio beyond human hearing is removed, or a quiet sound when followed by a loud sound.

MP4 is short for MPEG-4 part 14 and is video container format that encloses a video stream usually encoded using H264/5, and an audio stream encoded using MP3 or AAC. The MP4 format is commonly used for streaming video on the Internet and is supported by a wide range of video playback apps, hardware devices, and services.

MPEG stands for Moving Picture Experts Group and is a standards committee, supported by ISO, formed to establish uniform methodologies and algorithms for digital audio and video compression.

MPEG 1 Audio defined three different coding schemes for digitized audio, called Layers I, II, and III, utilizing psychoacoustics to reduce the amount of data. Layer I commonly known as MP1 encodes data at bit rates of 32 up to 448 Kbps and sampling frequencies of 32, 44.1 and 48 kHz. Layer II known as MP2, provides a higher compression efficiency with a sampling frequency of 192 to 256 Kbps for near CD quality audio. Layer III commonly known as MP3 provides a higher compression efficiency than Layer I & II, and can compress CD quality audio.

MPEG-1 Video standard was a video compression standard used in VideoCDs. MPEG-1 video offered resolutions of up to 352 × 240 at 29.97 fps and 352 × 288 at 25 fps with 24-bit colour and CD quality sound.

MPEG-2 Video standard offers resolutions of 720× 480 and 1280×720 at 60 fps, with full CD-quality audio. This is sufficient for all the major TV standards, including NTSC, and even HDTV. MPEG-2 is used by DVD-ROMs and is capable of compressing a 2 hour video into a few gigabytes.

MPEG-4 Video is a video compression method from the MPEG group, that was especially designed for low-bandwidth video/audio encoding purposes (less than 1.5Mbps). Not to be confused with MP4.

MPR2 provides reduced electrostatic and electromagnetic emissions. MPR 1990, or MPR2, is a standard defined to measure emissions from devices such as monitors.

MTBF is short for Mean Time Between Failure, the average time a specific component is expected to work without failure.

MTTR is short for Mean Time To Repair: the average time to repair a specific component.

Multi Mode fibre uses multiple light rays (or modes) through a 62.5 or 50 micron cable and can transmit up to 2 km.

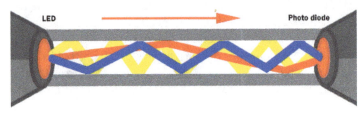

Here's a multimode ST patch cable. Notice the cables come in pairs. This is because the light signals travel in only one direction, so you need 1 cable to transmit, and one to receive.

Multi-Frequency is a monitor's ability to change resolution or refresh rate when signalled by a video adapter. Graphics cards can instruct a monitor to use various display resolutions and refresh rates. If the resolution or refresh rate is within a monitor's scanning range, multi-frequency monitors adjust to the resolutions and refresh rates set by the graphics card. Also known as multi-scanning.

Multilevel Feedback Queueing is a process scheduling system where each processes enters on the high priority queue. If a process uses too much CPU time, it is moved down to a lower-priority queue.

Processes on the lower queues are not serviced until all processes in the queues above are empty. The bottom queue uses a round robin scheduling scheme.

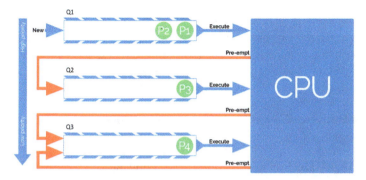

Multimedia refers to the delivery of information that combines different content formats (motion video, audio, still images, graphics, animation, text, etc.).

Multiplexer is a device that integrates serial digital waveforms into a single channel by partitioning the inputted data into segments and combining them together into a bitstream.

Multiprocessing is a single computer system with more than one physical CPU.

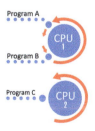

Multiscan is a monitor that can display many different resolutions. A single-scan monitor can only display a particular resolution.

Multitasking is the concurrent execution of multiple tasks, programs or processes. Pre-emptive multitasking uses a scheduling system where each running process receives a slice of time from the CPU. When it's time expires, the process is interrupted.

Multithreading is multiple concurrent threads of execution within a single application.

Multi-Timbral is the number of simultaneous instruments a synthesiser can play.

Munsell Colour System is a system consisting of over 3 million observations of what people perceive to be like differences in hue, chroma, and intensity. The participants chose the samples they perceived to have like differences.

MX Record is a record on a DNS server that points to the mail server responsible for dealing with email messages sent to a domain.

MySQL pronounced "My Sequel", or "My S.Q.L.", is an open-source relational database management system commonly used in web development. Many content management systems such as WordPress, Joomla, and Drupal use a MySQL database to store website data.

N

Nanometre nm: one thousand millionth of a metre.

Nanosecond ns: one thousand-millionths of a second of a second (.000000001 sec.). Light travels approximately 8 inches in 1 nanosecond.

NAND Flash is a type of non-volatile memory technology used in SSDs, USB flash drives, memory cards, and embedded systems.. The technology stores data in an array of memory cells made from floating-gate transistors.

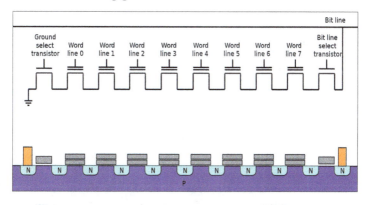

NAND flash offers high storage capacity, fast erase and write times, and lower cost per bit, but it has a limited number of write and erase cycles before the cells begin to wear out. To manage this, techniques such as wear levelling are used to extend the lifespan of NAND flash devices.

Napster was created in 1999 by Shawn Fanning and was a pioneering peer-to-peer file sharing system that gave users access to one each other's MP3 files to the dismay of the Recording Industry Association of America.

NAS Drive or Network Attached Storage (NAS) is a dedicated storage device connected to a network, allowing multiple users and devices to access and share files. NAS devices typically contain multiple hard drives or SSDs configured in RAID for redundancy and performance.

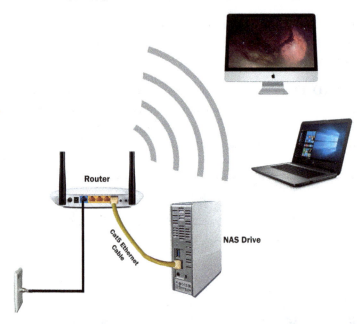

Natural Language Processing is a branch of artificial intelligence that focuses on the interaction between computers and humans through natural language. The objective is to enable computers to understand, interpret, and generate human languages. The technology combines computational linguistics—a rule-based modeling of human language—with statistical, machine learning, and deep learning models. This enables computers to process human language in the form of text or voice data and to 'understand' its full meaning. It is commonly used in a variety of applications, including language translation, speech recognition, voice-activated assistants such as Siri and Alexa, and in various chatbots.

NCQ stands for Native Command Queuing and is a technology designed to increase performance of SATA hard disks by allowing the disk firmware to internally optimise the order in which read and write commands are executed. For NCQ to be enabled, it must be supported and turned on in the SATA controller driver and in the hard drive itself.

NetBEUI stands for NetBIOS Extended User Interface, and was a networking protocol developed by IBM and Microsoft in 1985 for local area networks with up to 200 stations.

NetBIOS stands for Network Basic Input/Output System, was an interface developed by IBM in the 80s that allowed computers and devices to communicate over a network.

NetBIOS Name is a 15-character identifier used in older Windows networking to identify a computer and only work on local networks such as a LAN.

Network is a group of two or more computer systems linked together. There are many types of computer networks, including LANs MANs and WANs.

Network Address Translation (NAT) maps multiple private IP addresses to a public IP on the router in order to provide Internet access to the private hosts. NAT takes outbound packets from clients on the private network and translates the private IP into the public IP

Neural Network is a technology within the realm of machine learning. Drawing inspiration from the human brain's structure and functionality, a neural network is structured into layers comprising of an input layer, several hidden layers, and an output layer. Each layer contains interconnected nodes, or artificial neurons. Each connection has a specific weight and threshold. A node becomes activated and transmits data to the subsequent layer if its output surpasses a certain threshold value, facilitating the network's ability to process and analyze information.

NFC or Near Field Communication, is a short-range wireless communication technology that facilitates data exchange between devices within close proximity, typically within a range of a few centimeters. Operating at frequencies of 13.56 MHz, NFC enables contactless interactions, such as mobile payments, ticketing, and device pairing, by simply bringing NFC-enabled devices close together

Nginx, pronounced "engine-ex", is a high-performance open-source web server, reverse proxy, and load balancer. It is widely used for handling large numbers of concurrent connections efficiently.

NIC is short for Network Interface Card and is a card installed in a computer system to provide network communication capabilities to and from that computer.

Nit is a unit of luminance equal to one candlepower measured at a distance of 1m over an area of 1 square metre.

NLE stands for Non-Linear Editing and refers to the process of manipulating digitised video on a computer using specialised software such as Adobe Premiere, iMovie or Final Cut. The video clips can be cut, pasted and copied anywhere in the timeline of the project.

NLX is an Intel-designed motherboard form factor. It features a number of improvements over the ATX design providing support for new technologies such as AGP and allows easier access to motherboard components.

NMI stands for NonMaskable Interrupt and is a high-priority interrupt used to report malfunctions such as parity, bus and math co-processor errors.

NMOS stands for N-channel Metal Oxide Semiconductor and pertains to MOS devices constructed on a P-type substrate in which electrons flow between N-type source and drain contacts. NMOS devices are typically two to three times faster than PMOS devices.

Node is an endpoint of a network connection or a junction common to two or more lines in a network. Nodes can be processors, controllers, or workstations. The term is often used generically to refer to any entity that can access a network, and is frequently used interchangeably with device.

Noise is interference (or static) that disrupts the integrity of signals on communications lines. Noise can come from a variety of sources, including radio waves, nearby electrical wires, lightning, and bad connections. Noise is an analogue problem; once a signal is digitised, it is relatively immune to noise.

Nonce short for "number used once" is a randomly generated unique value that is used only once in cryptographic communication or protocol.

Non-Volatile Memory are types of memory that retain their contents when power is turned off. ROMs, PROMs, EPROMs and flash memory are examples. Sometimes the term refers to memory that is inherently volatile, but maintains its content because it is connected to a battery at all times, such as CMOS memory and to storage systems, such as hard disks.

North Bridge was a chipset component responsible for connecting the CPU to RAM and high-speed devices like PCIe graphics cards. In modern systems, its functions have been integrated into the CPU itself, eliminating the need for a separate North Bridge.

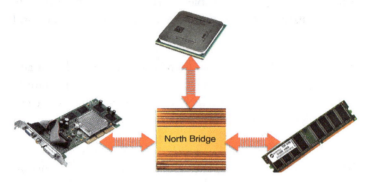

NOS stands for Network Operating System and is an operating system that include special functions for connecting computers and devices into a network. Some operating systems such as Windows and MacOS have networking functions built in. The term NOS is reserved for software that enhances a basic operating system by adding networking features.

NOT Gate has just one input. The NOT gate simply negates the input. So if the input is 1, the output is 0.

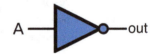

The truth table would be

A	Output
0	1
1	0

NTFS stands for New Technology File System, and is the file system native to Microsoft Windows. NTFS offers performance, compression, security, and the ability to handle large volumes and file sizes.

NTFS Permissions on the NTFS file system, is a set of permissions on a resource, file or folder that determine the access granted to a user, group or users, or a system processes. For example a user could have read only access to a shared folder, and full control of their own files.

NTP is a networking protocol for clock synchronization between computer systems over packet-switched, variable-latency data networks.

NTSC stands for National Television Standards Committee and is the industry group that formulated the standards for American television. An NTSC signal is a composite video signal used by televisions and VCRs in North America and some other parts of the world. The NTSC system uses 525 lines per frame, a field frequency of 60 Hz, a 30-frame per second update rate, and the YIQ colour space. Modern NTSC encoders and decoders may also use the YUV colour space.

NURBS stands for Nonuniform Rational B-Spline and is a type of spline that can represent more complex shapes than a Bezier spline.

NVidia CUDA (Compute Unified Device Architecture) is a parallel computing platform and application programming interface (API) model developed by Nvidia that allows software developers to use a CUDA-enabled graphics processing unit (GPU) for general purpose processing – an approach known as GPGPU (General-Purpose computing on Graphics Processing Units).

NVMe stands for Non-Volatile Memory Express and is a high-speed storage protocol using PCI express (x4) that was designed especially for SSDs. Drives that support this protocol have only one notch on the M.2 card connector (Key M).

NX stands for "No Execute" and is a joint venture hardware/software mechanism designed to defend against buffer overruns and consequent vulnerability to virus attack.

O

Object Oriented Programming, or OOP is a programming language that uses objects which contain data and code to develop software, rather than simply using functions and logic. Eg C++

OCR is short for Optical Character Recognition and is the electronic conversion of written or typed text into machine encoded text. Once converted the text can be edited.

ODBC short for Open Database Connectivity, and is a standard API that allows access to various database management programs such as DBASE, Microsoft Access, and Oracle using a common interface independent of the database file format. Using ODBC, you can write an application that uses the same code to read records from a DBASE file or a Microsoft Access Database

OEM is short for Original Equipment Manufacturer and refers to a manufacturer that builds systems or components used in another company's end product. For example, when a PC manufacturer builds a laptop and includes a pre-installed operating system like Microsoft Windows, the PC manufacturer is the OEM, while Microsoft is the software provider.

Off-Hook is a condition of a telephone line that corresponds to picking up the telephone receiver. A modem creates an off-hook condition when it tries to communicate on a telephone line.

OFTEL is the UK government regulator for telecommunications, first established in the 1980s to oversee the introduction of competition in a market dominated by British Telecom. Replaced by Ofcom in 2003.

OLE stands for Object Linking and Embedding and is an industry-standard method for inserting an object into a document. The document retains a connection, or link, with its original program so that double-clicking on the object in the document opens the object's original program. See also DLL.

OLED short for Organic Light-Emitting Diode and is a display device that uses sandwich carbon-based films between two charged electrodes - a metallic cathode and a transparent anode. The organic films consist of a hole-injection layer, a hole-transport layer, an emissive layer and an electron-transport layer.

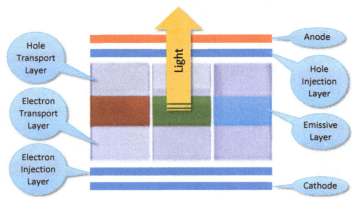

When voltage is applied to the OLED cell, the injected positive and negative charges recombine in the emissive layer and create electro luminescent light.

OneDrive is a file hosting and synchronization service developed by Microsoft that allow users to browse, view and organize files stored on their cloud storage space. OneDrive is integrated into Windows 10, with apps available for Android, iOS, as well as Xbox.

Opcode is the portion of a machine language instruction that specifies the operation to be performed. An opcode is critical in defining the instruction set of any processor, dictating how software controls hardware.

Operand is the data item (such as constants, variables, or expressions) that the operators act upon to perform a specific operation.

Open Type is a scalable font format developed jointly by Microsoft and Adobe, extending both the TrueType and PostScript font technologies. It supports advanced typographic features, better international character support, and cross-platform compatibility.

OpenGL stands for Open Graphics Library and is an open, cross-platform graphics API for rendering 2D and 3D graphics. Originally developed by Silicon Graphics (SGI), it is now maintained by the Khronos Group. OpenGL has been widely used in games, CAD, and virtual reality but is increasingly being replaced by Vulkan for modern high-performance applications.

Operating System or simply OS, is the software that controls the overall operation of a computer system, including such tasks as memory allocation, input and output distribution, interrupt processing, and job scheduling. The OS also provides a user interface for the user to interact such as GUI or CLI. MacOS, Windows, ChromeOS, iPadOS, iOS, Android and linux are common examples of operating systems.

Operator is a symbol or function that specifies an operation to be performed on one or more operands. For example: addition +, subtraction -, multiplication *, division /), comparison or relational operations (e.g., greater than >, less than <, equal to ==), logical operations (e.g., AND &&, OR ||, NOT !), assignment operations (e.g., assignment =, addition assignment +=).

Option ⌥ is a modifier key on macOS keyboards, used for alternative shortcuts, special characters, and system functions. While similar to the Alt key on Windows, the Option key has additional functions in macOS, such as entering special characters and accessing hidden menu items.

OR Gate has two inputs. An OR gates require either one or both inputs to be 1 for the output to be 1.

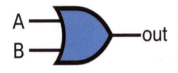

A	B	Output
0	0	0
0	1	1
1	0	1
1	1	1

OSI stands for Open System Interconnection and is an ISO standard for worldwide communications that defines a framework for implementing network protocols in seven layers. Information is passed down through the layers until it is transmitted across the network, where it is passed back up the stack to the application at the remote end.

OSI 7 Layer Model is a conceptual framework developed by the ISO to standardize networking protocols and functions. It defines seven layers that describe how data is transmitted over a network, from physical hardware (Layer 1) to application-level services (Layer 7). The OSI model divides the processes of a network into seven distinct layers, each with its own specific functions. These layers work together to facilitate the complete communication process.

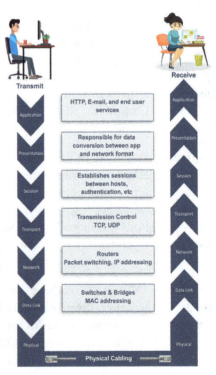

Overclock is to run a CPU or memory chip faster than its rated speed.

OverDrive is a digital lending platform that provides libraries and schools with access to eBooks, audiobooks, online magazines, and streaming media. It enables users to borrow digital content through library memberships. OverDrive is owned by Rakuten.

Overflow is a numerical answer that is too big for the allowed space to store

Overhead refers to the processing time required by the controller, host adapter, or drive prior to the execution of a command. Lower command overhead yields higher drive performance. Disk overhead refers to the space required for non- data information such as location and timing. Disk overhead often accounts for about ten percent of drive capacity. Lower disk overhead yields greater disk capacity.

Overlay is the ability to superimpose computer graphics over a live or recorded video signal and store the resulting video image on videotape. It is often used to add titles to videotape.

Overloading in programming, is the concept of having two or more functions with the same name but different parameters within the same scope. Overloading allows multiple behaviors for a function, differing by the type and/or number of arguments.

Overrun is the condition occurring when data is transmitted to a receiving device at a rate that's too fast for it to handle. See also Underrun and Flow Control.

Overscan is a condition that exists when a created image is larger than the visible portion of the display. Overscan helps relegate the relatively fuzzy perimeter of a CRT image to portions of the screen that are out of sight, and the overscan may disappear over time anyway. On the other hand, monitors with excessive overscan can lose icons and text at the edges of the display.

Overwrite is to write data over data already stored in a memory location.

P

P5 is Intel's codename for the original 60/66MHz Pentiums introduced in 1993. Subsequent faster clock-speed chips were referred to as P54 and the MMX version as P55.

P6 is Intel's codename for the Pentium Pro, which is optimised for 32-bit applications. The P6 generation includes the Pentium Pro and Pentium II.

PABX stands for Private Automatic Branch eXchange and is an in-house telephone switching system that interconnects telephone extensions to each other, as well as to the outside telephone network. Modern PBXs use all-digital methods for switching and can often handle digital terminals and telephones along with analogue telephones.

Packet is a basic unit of communication on a packet switched network that includes a header containing control information such as source and destination address, and a piece of the data being transmitted.

Version	Header Length	Type of Service	Total Length		
Identification			IP Flags	Fragment Offset	
Time to Live		Protocol	Header Checksum		
Source Address					
Destination Address					
IP Options					
Data/Message					

Packet Switching a network configuration where data is divided into small units called packets.

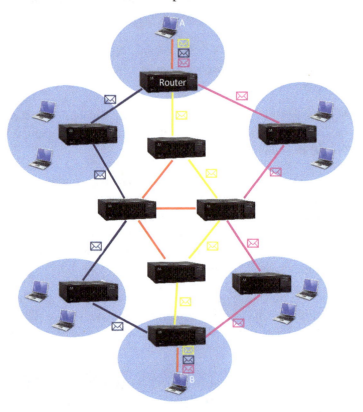

The data or message is divided up into multiple packets, for example, in the diagram above, the message is divided up into 3 packets (illustrated by the coloured envelopes in the diagram). Each packet is sent along a different route (illustrated by the coloured lines).

After reaching the destination through various different routes on the network, the packets are arranged in the original order according to the packet sequence number, there by reconstructing the message.

Page in DRAM memory, is the number of bits that can be accessed from one row address. The size of a page is determined by the number of column addresses. For example, a device with 10 column address pins has a page depth of 1024 bits.

Page Fault is a condition that occurs when a program tries to access a block of memory that is not currently stored in the computer's RAM. The operating system must then load the required data from disk to RAM, which can significantly slow down the process.

PAL is short for Phase Alternating Line and is a video format used in most of Western Europe, Australia and China as well as in various African, South American and Middle Eastern countries. PAL has a 4:3 image format, 625 lines per frame, a field frequency of 50Hz and 4 MHz video bandwidth with a total 8 MHz of video channel width. PAL has a 25-frame per second update rate and uses YUV colour space.

PAN is short for Personal Area Network and allows devices such as cellphones, headphones, tablets, mice, and keyboards to connect wirelessly within the one's personal space often using bluetooth.

PanelLink was developed by Silicon Images Inc. to provide an all digital link between a graphics card and an LCD monitor, PanelLink uses Transition Minimised Differential Signalling (TMDS) signalling technology, allowing a distance of up to 10m between the graphics card and the LCD panel.

Parameter refers to the variable in the declaration of a function or method that specifies the type of data it can accept, serving as a placeholder for arguments passed during execution.

Parallel Port is an I/O channel for a parallel device, like a printer, which sends and receives data eight bits at a time over 8 separate wires. Maximum throughput is around 500 Kbit/s.

Parallelogram Distortion is a type of geometric distortion, where lines are parallel but not perpendicular.

Parity is a data encoding scheme that devices use to check the validity of transmitted characters. This scheme adds an extra bit to each character, set by the transmitting computer based on the type of parity the computers agree to use (odd or even). For example, if the computers use even parity, the transmitting computer sets or clears the parity bit so that there are an even number of bits set in each character it transmits. The receiving computer checks each character and flags a parity error if any character has an odd number of bits set.

Parity Memory is a common method for ensuring the integrity of data stored in memory in which an additional data bit is generated and added to each data byte. Parity is able to detect only single bit errors reliably but cannot perform any correction. If more than one bit has been corrupted, the parity check may not detect a problem. The most commonly used forms of parity are even parity, odd parity, and checksums.

Particle Animation is rendering a 3D scene as millions of discrete particles rather than smooth, texture-mapped surfaces. Much more flexible but computer intensive.

Partition is a logical division of the storage area of a hard disk drive that can be managed separately.

Partition Table is the table located in the boot sector of a hard disk drive that lists all partitions on the disk.

Passive Matrix is a common LCD technology used in laptops. Passive matrix displays are not quite as sharp and do not have as broad a viewing angle as active matrix (TFT) displays.

222

Patch Cable is a short UTP cable usually used to connect patch panels to a network switch.

Patch Panel is a mountable panel that contains ports used to connect and manage LAN cables in a central point. From the front of the panel, the ports are usually 'patched in' to a core switch using a patch cable.

On the back of the panel, the Cat5 cables are terminated with a punch down or krone tool. These terminated cables run from another device such as a PC, printer, phone, or server, usually in another room or part of the building.

PCB is short for Printed Circuit Board and is a board printed with layers of circuits.

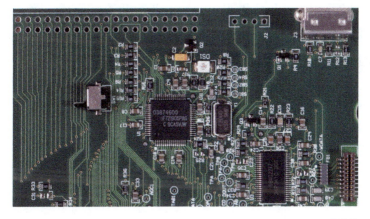

PCI stands for Peripheral Component Interconnect and is an industry-standard local bus for connecting peripheral devices to a computer's motherboard. Originally designed as a 32-bit bus, it also had 64-bit versions primarily used in servers and workstations. PCI was eventually replaced by PCI Express (PCIe), which offers greater bandwidth and scalability..

PCI Express short for Peripheral Component Interconnect Express and is a high speed industry-standard bus used for adding additional internal components such as graphics cards, and certain SSD drives to a computer. PCIe x16: has 16 lanes and is mainly used for high end graphics cards. PCIe x1: has 1 lane PCIe x4: has 4 lanes.

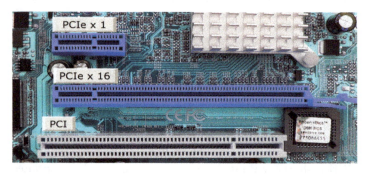

PCL short for Printer Control Language and is a protocol designed by Hewlett- Packard to allow PCs to communicate with its laser printers. PCL has become a de facto standard for laser and ink jet printers and is supported by virtually all printer manufacturers. "HP compatible

PCM short for Pulse Coded Modulation and is a technique for converting an analogue signal with an infinite number of possible values into discrete binary digital words that have a finite number of values. The waveform is sampled, then the sample is quantised into PCM codes. PCM is a digitisation technique used by the CCITT V.90 standard , not a universally accepted standard in its own right.

PCMCIA stands for Personal Computer Memory Card International Association and is a consortium of computer manufacturers that devised the standard for the credit card-size adapter cards used in many old notebook computers.

PCMCIA defines three card types:

- Type I cards can be up to 3.3mm thick and are generally used for RAM and ROM expansion cards
- Type II cards can be as thick as 5.5mm and typically house modems and fax modems
- Type III cards are the largest of the lot (up to 10.5mm thick) and are mostly used for solid state disks or miniature hard disks. PCMCIA cards are also known as PC Cards.

PCS stands for Personal Communications Services and is the collective term for US mobile telephone services in the 1900MHz frequency band.

PCX is a popular bitmapped graphics file format originally developed by ZSOFT for its PC Paintbrush program. PCX handles monochrome, 2-bit, 4-bit, 8-bit and 24-bit colour and uses Run Length Encoding (RLE) to achieve compression ratios of approximately 1.1:1 to 1.5:1.

PDA stands for Personal Digital Assistant and is a handheld device that combines computing, telephone/fax, and networking features. A typical PDA can function as a cellular phone, fax sender, and personal organiser. Some PDAs are hand-held PC with tiny keyboards. Another class of device uses a touch-screen and stylus for data entry.

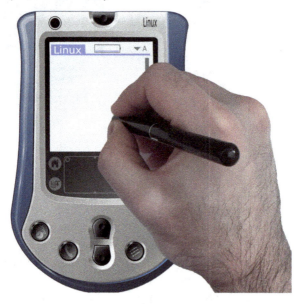

PDC stands for Personal Digital Cellular and is a Japanese standard for digital mobile telephony in the 800MHz and 1500MHz bands.

PDF stands for Portable Document Format and is a file format containing embedded fonts and graphics that is readable on various different operating systems and platforms.

PDL stands for Page Description Language and is a language for describing the layout and contents of a printed page used with laser printers. The best- known PDLs are Adobe PostScript and Hewlett-Packard PCL (Printer Control Language). Both PostScript and modern versions of PC

226

PDP stands for Plasma Display Panel and is a display technology that works on the principle that passing a high voltage through a low- pressure gas creates light.

Peer-to-Peer is a network architecture in which each workstation has equivalent capabilities and responsibilities. Contrast Client-Server.

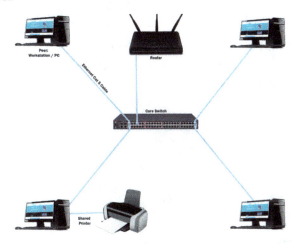

Performance is a measure of the speed of the drive during normal operation. Factors affecting performance are seek times, transfer rate, and command overhead.

Peripheral is a device connected to a computer that is external to the CPU. Examples include printers, cameras, mice, keyboards, scanners. As well as internal components such as hard disk drives and dvd drives.

Permalink is a permanent hyperlink or URL (Uniform Resource Locator) that points to a specific web page or resource on the internet often used in CMS such as wordpress or drupal.

Perspective Correction is the adjustment of texture maps on objects, viewed at an angle (typically large, flat objects) in order to retain the appearance of perspective.

227

PGA stands for Pin Grid Array and is a square chip package of either ceramic or plastic, with a high density of pins (typically 200 pins can fit in 1.5in square). In an SPGA (Staggered PGA), the pins are staggered and do not line up in perfect rows and columns.

Phantom Power is DC power transmitted through XLR cables to operate condenser microphones and other devices that contain active electronic circuitry. Usually 48-volt.

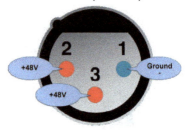

Pharming pronounced 'farming', this social engineering technique is designed to redirect a legitimate website's traffic to a duplicate fake site by either using the infected computer's hosts file, the victim's internet router, or a compromised DNS server.

Phishing pronounced 'fishing', this social engineering technique is designed to trick a user into handing over confidential information. Many phishing scams come via an email or phone call that appear to originate from a legitimate source, such as a bank, the police, IRS (HMRC), or a well known company.

Phosphor is a luminescent substance used to coat the inside of the cathode-ray tube display, that is illuminated by the electron gun in the pattern of graphical images as the display is scanned.

Phosphor Triad is one red, one green and one blue phosphor that composes a pixel.

Photolithography is the process of reproducing the chip's circuitry pattern onto the wafer surface by using ultraviolet light and stencils or masks to transfer the image photomechanically.

Photoresist is a material which becomes soluble when exposed to ultraviolet light. Used to help define circuit patterns during chip fabrication where it prevents etching or plating of the area it covers; also called resist.

PHP is short for Hypertext Preprocessor and is a widely-used open source scripting language used in web development. PHP code is processed on the web server by a PHP interpreter.

Physical Format is the actual physical layout of cylinders, tracks, and sectors on a disk drive.

Physical Modelling Synthesis is a revolutionary method for generating sound. This technique emulates the impulse patterns of real-world instruments using a software model.

PIC stands for Programmable Interrupt Controller and is a chip or device that prioritises interrupt requests generated by keyboards, serial ports, and other devices and passes them on to the CPU in order of highest priority. See also IRQ.

Picolitre pl: a million millionth of a litre.

Piezo-Electric is the property of certain crystals that causes them to oscillate when subjected to electrical pressure (voltage).

229

Pigment Inks consist of tiny chunks of solid pigment suspended in a liquid solution. According to their proponents, pigment inks offer richer, deeper colours and have less tendency to run, bleed or f

Pincushion Distortion is the opposite of barrel distortion. The vertical lines in a rectangular image curve inwards, with an increase in the distortion towards the edges of the image.

Ping is a network utility used to test the reachability of a host on an Internet Protocol (IP) network and to measure the round-trip time (RTT) for data packets sent from the originating host to a destination computer and back. The term "ping" originates from sonar technology, where a pulse of sound is sent out and the time it takes for the echo to return is measured.

PIO stands for Programmed Input Output Mode and is a method of transferring data to and from a storage device (hard disk or CD device) controller to memory via the computer's I/O ports, where the CPU plays a pivotal role in managing the throughput. For optimal performance a controller should support the drive's highest PIO mode (usually PIO mode 4).

Pipeline in DRAMs and SRAMs, is a method of increasing the performance using multistage circuitry to stack or save data while new data is being accessed. The depth of a pipeline varies from product to product. For example, in an EDO DRAM, one bit of data appears on the output while the next bit is being accessed. In some SRAMs, pipelines may contain bits of data or more.

Pipeline Burst Cache is a type of synchronous cache that uses two techniques to minimise processor wait states – a burst mode that pre- fetches memory contents before they are requested, and pipelining so that one memory value can be accessed in the cache at the same time that another memory value is accessed in DRAM.

Pipeline Processing is a category of techniques that provide simultaneous, or parallel, processing within a CPU. It refers to overlapping operations by moving data or instructions

Instruction	1	2			
Fetch					
Decode					
Execute					
Write					
Clock	1	2	3	4	5

into a conceptual pipe with all stages of the pipe processing simultaneously. For example, while one instruction is being executed, the computer is decoding the next instruction.

Pixel is an abbreviation for picture element and is the smallest unit of information in a digital image or display. Pixels are the individual points of colour that make up a digital image, viewed collectively to form pictures or videos on screens. The color and brightness of a pixel can vary, allowing for the wide range of visual effects seen in digital displays.

Pixel Clock Speed is the frequency or speed at which individual pixels (picture elements) in an image are written to the screen. The higher the pixel clock speed, the less flicker.

Pixelization is the graininess of an image that results when an image is enlarged. Also referred to as Pixelated.

Plated Media are the disks that are covered with a hard metal alloy instead of an iron-oxide compound. Plated disks can store more data than their oxide-coated counter-parts.

Platform is a computer system consisting of hardware and an operating system that a computer program can run on. The term often refers to a device's operating system such as Windows running on a PC, Android or iOS running on a smart phone, or MacOS running on a Mac.

Platter is a disk made of metal (or other rigid material) that is mounted inside a fixed disk drive. Most drives use more than one platter mounted on a single spindle (shaft) to provide more data storage surfaces in a smaller area.

PM stands for Phase Modulation and is a data transmission technique that encodes a data signal into a carrier by varying (or modulating) the phase of the carrier. The phase is the position of a single point on the wave.

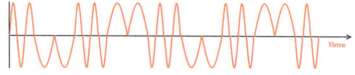

PMOS stands for P-channel Metal Oxide Semiconductor and pertains to MOS devices constructed on an N-type silicon substrate in which holes flow between source and drain contacts.

PnP stands for Plug and Play and is a Microsoft/Intel specification that allows for self-configuration of computer peripherals. Adding a PnP compliant device to a PnP enabled PC requires little more than making the physical connection. The operating system, in conjunction with PnP logic present in the BIOS and in the device itself, handles the IRQ settings, I/O addresses, and other technical aspects of the installation to ensure that the device does not conflict with other installed devices.

PoE stands for Power over Ethernet (PoE) is a standard for providing DC electrical power along with data over twisted pair ethernet cabling. There are two modes:

Mode A also known as endspan, transmits both data and power on the orange and green pairs. This method is best when both power and data originate from the same power sourcing equipment.

Mode B also known as midspan, transmits power over the blue and brown pairs and data on the orange and green pairs.

Mode A			**Mode B**		
Pin No.	Marking	Colour	Pin No.	Marking	Colour
1	Tx+ DC+		1	Tx+	
2	Tx – DC+		2	Tx –	
3	Rx+ DC-		3	Rx+	
4			4	PoE +	
5			5	PoE +	
6	Rx – DC-		6	Rx –	
7			7	PoE -	
8			8	PoE -	

PoE injectors that inject power into a standard Ethernet ports often use Mode B to power devices.

233

The power supply is usually between 44 – 57v, although 48v is used for most devices. PoE can be used to power wireless access points, VoIP phones, and IP cameras. PoE (802.3af) is the original PoE standard and provides 15.4W of power the device at 100m distance from the switch. PoE+(802.3at) provides 30W of power to the device at 100m distance from the switch. PoE++(802.3bt) doubles the PoE+ power to the device by providing 60W or 90W of power at 100m distance from the switch.

Polygon is any closed shape with four or more sides. In 3D, complex objects like teapots are decomposed, or "tessellated", into many primitive polygons to allow regular processing of the data, and hardware acceleration of that processing.

Polygon-Based Modelling is representing 3D objects as a set or mesh of polygons.

Polyphony is the number of voices a synthesiser can play at any one time.

Polysilicon is the conductive material used as an interconnect layer on a chip.

POP3 stands for Post Office Protocol, a standard email protocol used to retrieve emails from a remote server to a local email client. It typically downloads and deletes messages from the server after retrieval.

POSIX stands for Portable Operating System Interface for UNIX and is a set of IEEE and ISO standards that define an interface between programs and operating systems. By designing their programs to conform to POSIX, developers have some assurance that their software can be easily ported to POSIX-compliant operating systems. This includes most varieties of UNIX.

POST stands for Power-On Self-Test and is a set of diagnostic routines that execute when a computer is first powered on.

PostScript is a page description language developed by Adobe. Generally used by laser printers, PostScript is becoming increasingly common in high-end inkjets too.

POTS stands for Plain Old Telephone Service and is the basic analogue telephone service with no added features, such as call waiting or call forwarding.

Power Cycling is the act of turning a device off and then on again, which is often used as a troubleshooting step to reset systems and resolve software issues.

PPP stands for Point to Point Protocol and is a protocol that operates at layer 2 allowing data communication between two network entities or points. PPP is used by Internet service providers (ISPs) to enable connections to the Internet.

PPPoA is short for Point-to-Point Protocol over ATM and is a protocol that operates at layer 2 commonly used to connect domestic broadband modems to an ISP via telephone line.

PPPoE is short for Point-to-Point Protocol over Ethernet and is a network protocol for encapsulating Point-to-Point Protocol frames inside Ethernet frames.

Prefetch Unit is the unit that decides when to order data and instructions from the Instruction Cache, or the computer's main memory based on commands or the task being executed. When the instructions come in, the prefetch unit makes sure all the instructions are lined up correctly to send off to the decode unit.

Pretexting is a social engineering technique that uses a fabricated scenario designed to gain a user's trust and trick them into handing over personal information. This scam is usually a phone call that appears to come from an authority such as the police or tax office, but could also impersonate a co-worker, an insurance company, some fake organisation running bogus special offers, or some external IT support company.

Primitives are the smallest units in the 3D graphics usually points, lines, and polygons representing basic geometric shapes, such as spheres, cubes, and cylinders. Some 3D hardware and software schemes also employ curves, known as "splines".

Printer is a peripheral device used to make hard copy representations of graphics, photos or text on paper.

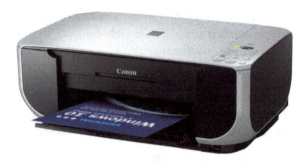

Printer Dot is the individual pixel in a halftone image. The size of a printer dot is variable, ranging from zero (all white) to the size of the halftone screen (all black).

PRML stands for Partial Response Maximum Likelihood and is a technique used to differentiate a valid signal from noise which achieves improved accuracy by looking at entire waveforms rather than just peaks in isolation, using digital signal processing (DSP) to reconstruct recorded data. On magnetic disks PRML uses RLL encoding to provide a ratio of user data to recorded data of 8:9.

Process Colours are the four primary ink colours Cyan, Magenta, Yellow and Black (CMYK) used in colour printing.

Protected Mode is a memory-addressing system used in 286 and later processors that prevents executing programs from overwriting one another in memory. Each program is allocated its own section of memory.

Protocol is a formal set of rules and descriptions that allow two computers to exchange information.

Proxy, in the context of networking, is a server (or a software system on a server) that acts as an intermediary between a client device, such as a computer, and the internet. It processes requests from the client to access resources on the internet, and depending on the type of proxy, it can provide various functionalities such as anonymity, security, content filtering, and caching. By routing the client's requests through the proxy server, the proxy can hide the client's IP address, enforce policies, or cache content for quicker access on subsequent requests.

PS/2 is an IBM personal computer series introduced in 1987, superseding the original PC line.

PSK stands for Phase Shift Keying is a data transmission technique that blends a data signal into a carrier by varying (modulating) the phase of the carrier by a certain number of degrees for each succeeding signal.

PSTN is short for Public Switched Telephone Network and is the global network of circuit-switched telephone systems that provides voice communication. While originally designed for analogue calls, modern PSTN includes digital services such as ISDN (Integrated Services Digital Network).

PSU is short for Power Supply Unit and is the component inside the computer that supplies power to the motherboard and internal drives.

Psychoacoustics is the study of how the human brain perceives sound. Findings relating to which sounds are and are not heard by the human ear have been used in the formulation of various audio compression techniques, including MP3.

Pulse Dialling is a method of dialling the telephone where the modem sends pulses (which you hear through the handset as clicks) to represent the telephone numbers (one pulse for a one, two pulses for a two, etc.). Pulse dialling is normally associated with rotary-dial phones. See also Tone Dialling.

PVR stands for Personal Video Recorder and is a generic term for the modern-day replacement of the VCR. Using hardware-based MPEG-2 compression like that used by DVDs, PVRs encode video data and store the data on a hard disk drive. PVRs have all of the functionality of VCRs, (recording, playback, fast forwarding, rewinding, pausing) plus the ability to instantly jump to any part of the program without having to rewind or fast forward the data stream. Also referred to a Digital Video Recorder.

Python is a high-level, interpreted programming language known for its simplicity, readability, and versatility. It supports multiple programming paradigms, including procedural, object-oriented, and functional programming. Python is widely used in various fields such as web development, data science, artificial intelligence (AI), automation, and scientific computing. First released in 1991 by Guido van Rossum, Python is designed to emphasize code clarity and ease of use, making it a popular choice for both beginners and experienced developers. Its vast ecosystem includes a rich standard library and an extensive collection of third-party packages, enabling rapid development of applications. Python has undergone major evolutions, with Python 2 (deprecated in 2020) and Python 3 (the current standard). Python's design philosophy, summarized by the Zen of Python, promotes simplicity, explicitness, and readability, making it one of the most widely adopted programming languages today.

Q

QAM is short for Quadrature Amplitude Modulation and is modulation technique used by high speed modems combining two amplitude-modulated (AM) signals into a single channel, thereby doubling the effective bandwidth.

QoS (Quality of Service) is a set of technologies and services that manage traffic on a network by prioritizing specific types of data, ensuring the performance of critical applications and services despite potential congestion on the network.

QR Code (Quick Response Code) is type of two-dimensional barcode that can be read using smartphones and dedicated QR reading devices, that links directly to text, emails, websites, phone numbers, and more. QR codes are used for quick access to device information and to facilitate actions like tracking inventory or accessing a website without having to type in a URL.

Quantisation is the process of representing a voltage with a discrete binary digital number. Approximating an infinite valued signal with a finite number system introduces an error called quantisation error or noise.

Quantum Computing is a revolutionary approach to computation that uses principles of quantum mechanics to process information. Unlike classical computing, which uses bits as the smallest unit of data (represented as either 0 or 1), quantum computing uses quantum bits, or qubits, which can exist in multiple states simultaneously allowing a qubit to be in a state of 0, 1, or both 0 and 1 at the same time. This capability is a key factor that enables quantum computers to perform complex calculations and process vast amounts of data much more efficiently than classical computers.

Qubit (Quantum Bit) is the basic unit of quantum information which can exist in multiple states simultaneously and be in a state of 0, 1, or both 0 and 1 at the same time.

Queue is an abstract data structure in which items are stored in order. See FIFO and LIFO. Also an area where processes await their turn to be executed by a CPU.

QuickTime is Apple Computer's multimedia framework for processing video, audio and pictures.

Quota is a limit set on the amount of resources a user or system can consume such as disk space, CPU usage, or network bandwidth.

QWERTY is the most widely used keyboard layout for Latin-script alphabets, named after the first six letters in the top row.

Designed in the 1870s by Christopher Latham Sholes for manual typewriters, its primary goal was to reduce mechanical jamming by spacing out frequently used letter pairs. The layout gained widespread adoption after being used in Remington typewriters and later became the standard for computer keyboards. Despite the existence of alternative layouts like Dvorak and Colemak, QWERTY remains dominant due to familiarity and global standardization. It has also been adapted for modern digital devices, virtual keyboards, and predictive text systems.

R

RADIUS stands for Remote Authentication Dial-In User Service protocol and is a client/server security protocol that allows network managers to centralise user authentication on a single server. This means users can use one set of network credentials to access various network resources such as a WiFi network, NAS drive share and so on.

RADSL stands for Rate Adaptive Digital Subscriber Line and is an implementation of ADSL that automatically adjusts the connection speed on start up to adjust for the quality of the telephone line, thereby allowing the service to function over longer distances than does ordinary ADSL.

RAID, an acronym for Redundant Array of Independent Disks and is a data storage technology that combines multiple physical disk drives into one or more logical units for the purposes of data redundancy, performance improvement, or both. RAID can be implemented through software or hardware, with multiple levels of configuration, each offering a different balance between performance, data protection, and capacity efficiency.

RAID 0 (Striping) enhances performance by splitting data evenly across two or more disks with no redundancy, offering improved speed but no fault tolerance. Ideal for environments where performance is more critical than data redundancy, such as non-critical applications, gaming systems, and image editing workstations.

RAID 1 (Mirroring) offers redundancy by duplicating the same data on two or more disks. This ensures data availability and fault tolerance but requires more storage capacity. Suitable for mission-critical applications.

RAID 5 (Striping with Parity) distributes data and parity information across three or more disks. It offers a balance between performance, storage efficiency, and fault tolerance. If one disk fails, the system can rebuild the lost data using the parity information. Well-suited for file and application servers, medium-sized databases

RAID 6 (Striping with Double Parity) is similar to RAID 5 but adds an extra layer of parity data, allowing it to withstand the failure of two disks without losing data. This level requires at least four disks and provides greater fault tolerance at the cost of additional storage space for the second parity block. Best used in environments where data availability and fault tolerance are extremely critical

RAID 10 (1+0) combines the mirroring of RAID 1 with the striping of RAID 0. It offers high performance and fault tolerance by mirroring each disk in the RAID 0 array. This level requires at least four disks and is well-suited for databases and applications that require high performance and reliability. Ideal for high-performance computing environments that require maximum speed and reliability, such as high-traffic web servers.

RAID 50 (5+0) combines the advantages of RAID 5's parity-based fault tolerance with RAID 0's performance. This configuration requires at least six disks and is typically used in large, mission-critical environments where both high performance and data integrity are required. Suitable for large, mission-critical applications that require a balance of high performance and increased data protection.

RAID 60 (6+0) merges RAID 6's double parity feature with RAID 0's striping. It offers very high fault tolerance and can survive the loss of two disks in each RAID 6 subset. This setup is suitable for very large storage solutions where data availability and integrity are paramount. Utilized in very large storage environments that demand the highest levels of data protection.

Rainbow Effect is an artefact unique to single-chip DLP projectors which appears as a rainbow or multi-colour shimmer briefly noticeable by some people when they change focus from one part of the projector screen to another. It appears as a secondary image that appears at the viewer's peripheral vision and is typically noticeable when shifting focus from a high contrast area or bright object.

RAM stands for Random Access Memory and is the primary storage location used to store working data and program code in a computer system. Each memory location can be accessed directly. RAM is volatile, meaning the data is lost when the power is cut.

RAM Disk is a virtual drive created by setting aside a section of RAM and accessed as if it were a disk drive. Access to a RAM disk is very fast but data is lost when the system is reset or turned off.

RAMDAC converts the data in the frame buffer into the RGB signal required by the monitor.

Random Access is the ability to access any particular block by going directly to it. Memory and disk devices support random access; by contrast, tape storage devices do not.

Ransomware is a type of malicious software designed to block access to a computer system or encrypt files until a sum of money, or ransom, is paid. Ransomware  typically spreads through phishing emails containing malicious attachments, compromised websites, or exploiting vulnerabilities in software. Once installed, it can lock the system's screen or encrypt crucial files with a key known only to the attacker.

Victims are usually given instructions on how to pay the ransom in cryptocurrency to regain access to their data. Even if the ransom is paid, there is no guarantee that the data will be decrypted or restored. Ransomware attacks can target individuals, businesses, and government agencies, leading to significant financial losses, data breaches, and disruption of operations. Preventative measures include regular backups, and educating users on the risks of phishing emails.

RAS stands for Row Address Select (or Strobe) and is a control pin on DRAM memory used to latch and activate a row address. The row selected is determined by the data present at the address pins when RAS becomes active.

RAS Line is a physical track on motherboard used to select which sides of which SIMMs will be involved in a data transfer. A given chipset supports only a certain number of RAS lines, thereby dictating how many SIMMs can be accommodated. A pair of SIMMs uses one RAS line; a pair of DIMMs uses two.

Raspberry Pi is a series of small single-board computers developed in the United Kingdom by the Raspberry Pi Foundation to promote teaching of basic computer science in schools and in developing countries.

Raster is a rectangular grid of picture elements representing graphical data for display. Raster operations (ROPs) can be performed on some portion or all of the raster.

Raster Image is grid-based image composed of individual pixels, commonly used in formats like PNG, BMP, and JPEG. Unlike vector graphics, raster images lose quality when scaled.

Rasterization is the process of converting vector-based graphics or 3D models into a raster image by determining pixel values based on the objects' color, shading, and lighting.

Rate Limiting is process of controlling the rate of traffic sent or received by a network interface, typically used to prevent spamming, denial-of-service attacks, and to manage network congestion.

RCA stands for Radio Corporation of America and refers to the standard single ended analogue cables used to connect audio and video devices together.

Typically red/white inputs are for the left/right channels of sound and yellow is for video.

Read After Write is a mode of operation that has the computer read back each sector immediately after it is written on the disk, checking that the data read back is the same as recorded. This slows disk operations, but raises reliability.

Read Channel is a circuit on a hard disk drive that converts the digital data into magnetic flux changes for recording to the disk's magnetic surface, and vice versa.

Read Verify is a disk mode where the disk reads in data to the controller, but the controller only checks for errors and does not pass the data on to the system.

Recovery Console is a command-line utility integrated into Microsoft Windows 2000 and XP, designed to help diagnose and repair system problems. It provides a limited set of administrative commands that allow users to access the filesystem, format drives, read and write data on the local hard drive, and perform other tasks from a command prompt. The Recovery Console is particularly useful for fixing boot problems, replacing system files, managing partitions, and performing other recovery operations when Windows cannot start normally. It has been replaced by Windows Recovery Environment (WinRE) in later versions of Windows.

Read/Write Head is the part of a hard disk drive responsible for encoding (writing) and decoding (reading) data on the spinning magnetic platters. Modern drives use magneto-resistive (MR) or giant magneto-resistive (GMR) heads for increased sensitivity and precision.

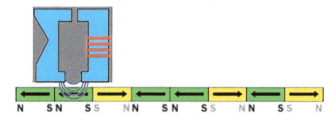

Heads come in many different shapes and forms, and are used for both contact and non- contact type recording. Here below is an example of a read/write head in a hard disk drive.

246

Real Audio is an audio compression scheme used on the Internet to provide streamed audio.

Real-time refers to an operating mode under which data is received and processed and the results returned so quickly as to seem instantaneous.

Rear Projection the projector is placed behind a translucent screen. See also Front Projection.

Recursion is a programming technique where a function calls itself directly or indirectly in order to solve a problem. It breaks down a complex problem into simpler or smaller versions of the same problem, known as recursive cases, and solves them with recursive calls. Recursion continues until it reaches a base case, a condition under which it can return a result without making any further recursive calls. This approach is particularly useful for tasks that can be defined in terms of similar subtasks, such as traversing data structures (eg trees), implementing algorithms (such as sorting and searching), and solving mathematical problems (like calculating factorials or Fibonacci numbers).

Reed-Solomon is an error-correction encoding system that cycles data multiple times through a mathematical transformation in order to increase the effectiveness of the error correction, especially for burst errors (ie errors that occur closely together such as a physical defect).

Reflections are sounds that originate from a sound source and bounce off walls, floors, ceilings and other obstructions before reaching the listener.

Refresh is the process used to restore the charge in DRAM memory cells at specified intervals. The required refresh interval is a function of the memory cell design and the semiconductor technology used to manufacture the memory device. There are several refresh schemes that may be used.

Refresh Rate is expressed in Hertz (Hz), and in interlaced mode is the number of fields written to the screen every second. In non-interlaced mode it is the number of frames written to the screen every second. Higher frequencies reduce flicker, because they light the pixels more frequently, reducing the dimming that causes flicker. Also called vertical frequency.

Regedit is short for Registry Editor and is a Windows utility that allows users to view, search for, and modify the Windows Registry, a hierarchical database that stores app settings, user and device configurations for Microsoft Windows.

Registered Memory is a type of SDRAM memory that uses registers to hold data for one clock cycle before it is moving it on and in so doing increases the reliability of high-speed data access. Registered memory modules are typically used only in server environments and other mission-critical systems. Registered and unbuffered memory cannot be mixed. the design of the processor's memory controller dictating which type is required.

Registers are mini-storage areas for data used by the Arithmetic Logic Unit (ALU) to complete the tasks the Control Unit has requested. The data can come from the data cache, main memory or the control unit and are all stored at special locations within the Registers. This makes retrieval for the ALU quick and efficient.

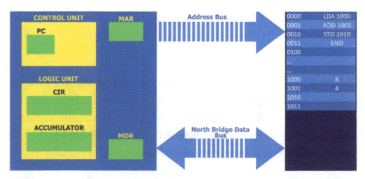

Registry is a hierarchical database used to store configuration information in Windows. See Regedit

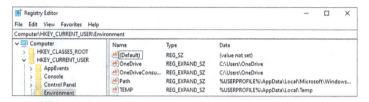

Relational Database is a structured database model that organizes data into one or more tables, often referred to as "entities". These tables are composed of rows and columns, with each row representing a unique record and each column representing a specific field within the record. In this model, a primary key uniquely identifies each record within a table, ensuring data integrity and facilitating efficient retrieval.

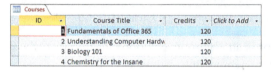

Relationships between tables are established through foreign keys, which reference the unique primary key in another table. For example, in a database for a university, the student table may be linked to the transcript table through a foreign key relationship.

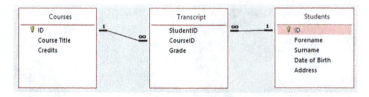

Popular relational database management systems (RDBMS) that adhere to the principles of the relational model include Microsoft Access, MySQL, PostgreSQL, Oracle Database, and Microsoft SQL Server.

Removable Storage is any storage type that allows the actual storage media to be removed from the computer or drive, such as a CD/DVD, tape, memory card, flash drive, or external hard disk. It is used for the transportation of data between computers and for data backup.

Rendering is the drawing of an effect or scene as it appears.

Request To Send or simply **RTS** is an RS-232C signal that requests the modem to send data. It initiates any data transmission between the computer (or terminal) and the modem. It is answered by a Clear To Send (CTS) signal.

Resistor is an electronic component that resists the flow of current in an electronic circuit.

Resolution is the number of pixels per unit of area, usually measured in pixels or dots per inch. The finer the grid defining an area, the more pixels it contains and the higher its resolution. The higher the resolution the greater its detail.

19" @ 800x600   19" @ 1024x768

250

Response Time when referring to LCD monitors is the time it takes for the liquid crystal inside a screen panel to respond to applied current. Also the time it takes for a component to respond to a command.

Responsive Design is a web design approach aimed at building websites that provide an optimal viewing experience across a wide range of devices and screen sizes (from desktop computer monitors and tablets to mobile phones).

REST API (Representational State Transfer Application Programming Interface) is an architectural style and approach to communications often used in web services development. REST APIs enable two computer systems to exchange information securely and efficiently over the internet by adhering to stateless communication protocols. This approach is particularly beneficial for applications that require interaction with other internal or external applications to perform tasks. For instance, generating monthly payslips may involve an internal accounting system communicating with a bank's system to process payments and integrating with an internal timesheet application for accurate billing. By following standardized HTTP methods (GET, POST, PUT, DELETE), REST APIs facilitate this seamless integration, promoting secure, reliable, and efficient data exchange between disparate systems. This standardization ensures that developers can create interoperable web services that can easily scale and adapt to meet evolving business needs.

Reverb or Reverberation is the sum of all sound reflections or echoes in a given environment.

RF stands for Radio Frequency and is the range of electromagnetic frequencies above the audio range and below visible light. All broadcast transmission, from AM radio to satellites, falls into this range, which is between 30KHz and 300GHz.

RGB short for Red-Green-Blue, an additive colour model for displaying images in computer graphics by describing the amount of each of the three primary colours: Red, Green and Blue. Three bytes are required for "true colour" (three numbers between 0 and 255), giving a theoretical maximum of 16.7 million colours.

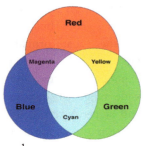

RIAA stands for Recording Industry Association of America: The association formed by the recording companies in the United States to promote the recording industry and to defend its legal rights. The RIAA equalisation curve is a compensation method applied to a signal from a record deck pick-up. Phono pre-amps have RIAA circuitry built-in.

RIFF stands for Resource Interchange File Format and is a platform-independent multimedia specification (published by Microsoft and others in 1990) that allows audio, image, animation, and other multimedia elements to be stored in a common format. See also Media Control Interface (MCI).

RIMM stands for Rambus in-line memory module, a memory module similar to DIMMs.

Ripper is the name given to the specialised software that extracts raw audio data from a music CD. The ability to extract audio digitally relies on a feature of newer CD-ROM drives that allows the digital data from audio CDs to be passed through the computer's bus (IDE, SCSI) just like CD-ROM data.

RISC stands for Reduced Instruction Set Computer. RISC processors use simple instructions that are executed within one clock cycle. RISC instructions operate only on processor registers and are fast.

```
LDA 1000
ADD 1001
STO 1010
```

This processor architecture is used in cellular smartphones and some computer tables.

RJ11 is a common jack type most often used for connecting analogue phones, modems, and fax machines to a phone line. Contains 6 wires but only the middle 2 are normally used for a single device.

RJ45 stands for Registered Jack (RJ) number 45 and is a standardized network interface for connecting data devices such as computers, ethernet switches and routers. Twisted pair Ethernet cables are terminated with a standard RJ45 connector.

Each of the wires is inserted into an RJ45 plug using either the T-568A spec, or more commonly the T-586B spec, as shown below:

Twisted pair cabling is comprised of two independently insulated wires twisted around each other in varying degrees of twist. The

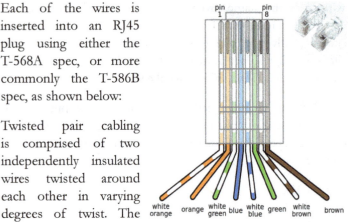

orange pair is twisted more tightly than the brown pair. This helps to counteract noise and interference. These cables come in unshielded (UTP) and shielded (STP) versions. Devices are connected individually to a switch, so if one connection fails, the rest of the network can continue to operate.

RLE stands for Run Length Encoding and is a lossless data compression algorithm usually used to compress repetitive data. The compression process involves counting the number of consecutive occurrences of each character (called a run).

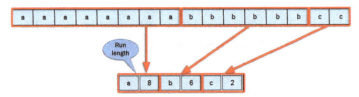

RLL short for Run Length Limited and is a method used on some hard disks to encode data into magnetic pulses. RLL requires more processing, but stores almost 50 percent more data per disk than the older MFM (modified frequency modulation) method. The run length is the maximum number of consecutive 0s before a 1 bit is recorded.

Roaming is the ability of a cellular customer to automatically make and receive voice calls, send and receive data, or access other services when traveling outside the geographical coverage area of their home network, by using a visited network.

Roland GS is Roland General Synthesiser and General MIDI two overlapping specifications for defining the standard sets of MIDI sounds that are associated with specific commands.

ROM stands for Read Only Memory and is a type of non-volatile memory that stores firmware or permanent data. ROM retains its data even when the system is powered off. Some types, such as EEPROM and Flash ROM, can be rewritten, while others, like Mask ROM, are permanently programmed during manufacturing.

Root Certificate is a public certificate issued by a trusted certificate authority (CA) that identifies the CA. Root certificates are at the base of a digital certificate chain, which is used for secure communication on the internet.

Root Directory (also called root folder) is the topmost directory in a file system hierarchy, from which all other directories branch off. In UNIX and Linux systems, it is denoted as "/", while in Windows, it can be represented by the drive letter followed by a backslash (e.g., "C:\").

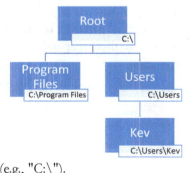

Rooting is the process of gaining root (superuser) access on a device, allowing users to modify system files, install custom firmware (ROMs), and remove pre-installed restrictions. Rooting also bypasses security measures and may void warranties.

Rootkit is a program designed to enable unauthorised, remote administrator access to a computer by opening a backdoor. Rootkits don't replicate themselves like worms and viruses do and are usually installed through phishing attacks, executable files, security exploits, or software downloaded from a dodgy website. Once installed, an attacker can connect to the infected machine and introduce other malware to steal information. Rootkits usually hide themselves on the infected machine and can be difficult to detect.

Root-Level refers to the highest level of access or permission available in a system, particularly in Unix and Linux environments. Having root-level access means having the permissions to perform any operation on the system, akin to being an administrator.

Root Zone in a DNS (Domain Name System) hierarchy, the root zone is the top-level of the DNS structure. It contains the authoritative database of all top-level domain names (such as .com, .net, .org, etc.), managed by a root server.

Round Robin Scheduling is a process scheduling system where each process is given a fixed amount of execution time (quantum). A process is executed until its time expires. This process is then suspended, and the next process begins its execution.

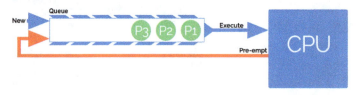

When all the processes in the queue have been allocated an amount of time, the scheduler returns to the beginning of the process queue and starts again.

Router is a layer 3 network device that forwards data packets between different networks, directing traffic based on IP addresses. Enterprise routers manage traffic on larger networks, and often have security features like firewalls. At home or in a small office, the device that connects your laptop, tablet, or smartphone to the internet is called a router.

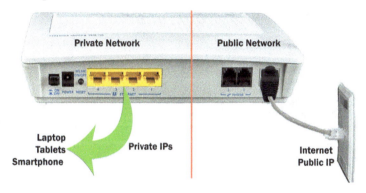

Routing Table is data table stored in a router or a networked computer that lists the routes to particular network destinations. The table contains information about the topology of the network immediately around it.

Row is part of the RAM array. A bit is stored where a column and a row intersect.

RPC is short for Remote Procedure Call, a protocol that enables a program to request services from another computer on a network or the internet.

RPM stands for Revolutions Per Minute and is the number of complete rotations in 1 minute. RPM is used as a measure of rotational speed. RPM = number of revolutions / minutes

RS-232 is a serial communication standard established by the Electronic Industries Association (EIA) for transmitting data between data terminal equipment (DTE), such as a computer or terminal, and data communication equipment (DCE), such as a modem. It defines voltage levels, baud rates, signal timing, and handshaking protocols for serial communication over a point-to-point connection. RS-232 was widely used for connecting peripheral devices, including modems, printers, and industrial equipment, but has largely been replaced by faster interfaces like USB and Ethernet. Despite this, it remains in use for legacy systems, embedded systems, and industrial automation.

RTF short for Rich Text Format: a format commonly used by most word processors that contains the text, formatting, images, and page layout.

RRT (Rount Trip Time) is the time it takes for a signal to travel from the origin to a destination plus the time it takes for an acknowledgment of that signal to return to the origin. RTT is a key factor in determining the efficiency of network communication.

Ryzen is a series of microprocessors developed by AMD, designed to compete with Intel's Core series (i3, i5, i7, i9) and Xeon processors. Ryzen processors are known for their multi-core performance, energy efficiency, and suitability for gaming, professional workloads, and high-performance computing.

S

S/PDIF stands for Sony/Philips Digital Interchange Format and is an interface standard used to connect consumer audio equipment using either coaxial cable with RCA connectors or optical cable with TOSLINK connectors.

Sampling is the process of converting an analogue signal into a digital representation. This is accomplished by measuring the value of the analogue signal at regular intervals called samples. These values are then encoded to provide a digital representation of the analogue signal.

Sampling Rate is the frequency with which samples are taken and converted into digital form. The sampling frequency should be at least twice that of the analogue frequency being digitised. Thus, the sampling rate for hi-fi playback is 44.1kHz, slightly more than double the 20kHz frequency humans can hear.

SAN stands for Storage Area Network and is a high-speed special purpose network containing disk arrays for data storage and provides a shared pool of storage space. Each user connected to a SAN can access that data as if it were a local disk connected directly to the computer.

Sandbox is a security mechanism for separating running programs, often used to execute untested code, or untrusted programs from unverified third-parties, suppliers, untrusted users, and untrusted websites.

SAS stands for Serial Attached SCSI, and is a serial interface for connecting high speed hard drives to a computer, replacing old parallel SCSI.

The drive is connected using a SAS drive cable.

SATA stands for **S**erial **A**dvanced **T**echnology **A**ttachment. SATA is an interface that connects mass storage devices such as hard drives, solid-state drives and other types of drive to a computer's motherboard. SATA is based on serial signalling technology, a single cable with a minimum of four wires creating a point-to-point connection between devices.

The drive is connected using a SATA data cable and a SATA power cable.

260

Saturated Colours are strong, bright colours (particularly reds and oranges) which do not reproduce well on video; they tend to saturate the screen with colour or bleed around the edges, producing a garish, unclear image.

Saturation is the intensity of a colour or hue. For example, a fully saturated blue would be a pure, bright blue. A less saturated blue, the more pastel the appearance. See also Chroma.

SCA stands for Single Connector Attachment and is the same speed SCSI interface as LVD, but integrates power and I/O information into a single 80-pin connector. Used in high-end servers to allow hard disks to be hot- swapped in a RAID array.

Scalability is the ability to vary the information content of a program by changing the amount of data that is stored, transmitted or displayed. In a video image, this translates into creating larger or smaller windows of video on screens (shrinking effect).

Scaling the process of changing the size of characters or graphics.

Screen Door Effect (SDE) is common with LCD-based projectors and relates to a viewer's awareness of the grid, or spacing between the pixels. The lines which form the grid are, in fact, where the panel's control electronics are preventing light from shining through the panel.

Screen Regulation is a distortion where the size of the image varies according to the brightness of the screen content. A white rectangle will appear larger when surrounding a solid white rectangle than when surrounding a plain black area.

Scripting Language is a programming language that supports scripts, programs written for a special run-time environment that automates the execution of tasks that could alternatively be executed one-by-one by a human operator. Scripting languages are often interpreted, rather than compiled.

SCSI stands for Small Computer System Interface and is a parallel interface for attaching disk drives, scanners, printers, and other peripherals to a computer. Internal SCSI disk drives were attached to a host controller using a 68 pin ribbon cable.

You could connect up to 15 devices to a host controller creating a SCSI chain. External SCSI devices used a 50 pin cable

SD Card stands for Secure Digital Card and is a memory card commonly used in digital cameras, laptops, tablets, and phones to store data. They come in standard size and micro.

Standard SD   Micro SD   SD Card Adapter

SDK (Software Development Kit) is a collection of software development tools in one installable package. They facilitate the creation of applications by having compiler, debugger and perhaps a software framework. They are normally specific to a hardware platform and operating system combination.

SDLC stands Software Development Life cycle and is a methodology used to develop software: Analysis, design, implementation, testing, deployment.

SDMI stands for Secure Digital Music Initiative and is a secure digital format for distributing music over the Internet. Announced in February 1999, it was backed by the Recording Industry Association of America (RIAA) and Sony, Warner, BMG, EMI and Universal – the top five music production companies..

SDRAM Synchronous DRAM, a type of DRAM that delivers bursts of data at very high speeds synchronised by an external clock signal. See DDR., DRAM.

SDTV stands for Standard definition television, a television broadcast system with resolutions of 720 x 480, or 720 x 576. See HDTV

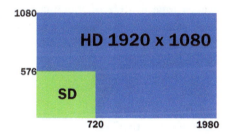

SEC or SECC short for Single Edge Contact Cartridge, and is a processor module first used by Intel's Pentium II CPU. It comprised of a hardware module that contained the CPU itself and an external L2 cache.

The module plugged into a slot (called Slot 1, Slot 2, or Slot A) on the motherboard .

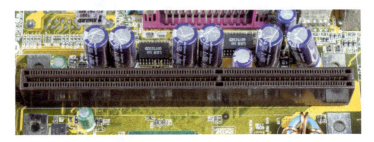

SECAM stands for Sequentiel Coleur A Memoire and is a video standard, used in France and Eastern Europe with image format 4:3, 819 lines per frame, 50 Hz and 6 MHz video bandwidth with a total 8 MHz of video channel width. Like the similar PAL standard, it has a 25-frame per second update rate. The major difference from PAL is that SECAM uses FM-modulated chrominance.

Sector is the minimum segment of track length that can be assigned to store data. Magnetic disks are typically divided into tracks, each which contains a number of sectors. A sector contains a predetermined amount of data, such as 512 bytes.

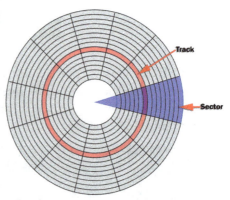

Secure Boot is a UEFI security feature designed to prevent unauthorized operating systems or malware from loading during startup. It ensures that only software with verified digital signatures from trusted vendors can be executed, thereby protecting the system against boot-time attacks.

Seek Time is the time taken for the actuator to move the heads to the correct cylinder in order to access data.

Semiconductor is a solid-state substance with conductive properties that can be altered with electricity. Silicon performs as a semiconductor when chemically combined with other elements. A semiconductor is also halfway between a conductor and an insulator. When charged with electricity or light, semiconductors change their state from non conductive to conductive or vice versa. The most significant product built from a semiconductor is the transistor.

Sequencer is software for recording and editing MIDI files.

SEO is short for Search Engine Optimization and is the process of optimizing web based content so that search engines such as Google can find and rank it according to a customer's search.

Serial Port is a connector that facilitate communication between a computer and a serial devices such as a modems,  plotter, or mouse, and other equipment. On a PC, this socket is a DB-9 male connector. It is a full-duplex device, using separate lines for transmitting and receiving data at the same time. Maximum throughput is 115.2 Kbit/s. Also called a COM or communications port.

Server is a computer program usually running on a large computer that delivers a service to other devices on a network. There are various types of server. A web server hosts websites and serves web pages. A file server stores and serves files. A mail server stores email accounts and messages.

Servo Motor is a motor used for precise control of angular and linear movements often used in robotics.

Settle Time is the interval between the arrival of the read/write head at a specific track, and the lessening of the residual movement to a level sufficient for reliable reading or writing.

Setup is the conversion of a set of instructions concerning the size, shape and position of polygons into a 3D scene ready for rasterization.

SGRAM stands for Synchronous Graphics RAM and is a single ported DRAM designed for high-speed, serial data, and usually used on graphics boards.

Shader is an algorithm which mathematically describes how an individual material is rendered to an object and how light interacts with its overall appearance.

Shading is the process of creating pixel colours. Gouraud is a constant increment of colour from one pixel to the next, while Phong is much more complex and higher quality. Flat shading means no smooth blending of colours, each polygon being a single colour.

Shadow Copy is a technology included in Microsoft Windows that allows taking manual or automatic backup copies or snapshots of computer files or volumes, even when they are in use. It is used to create restore points for the System Restore feature.

Shadow Mask is the perforated metal sheet that rests between the electron gun and a screen's phosphor coating to ensure that the three electron beams only strike the correct phosphor dots. A "shadow mask display" is a monitor which conforms to the conventional three- electron gun, shadow mask design.

Shannon's Law defines the relationship between the maximum throughput in any given channel to the presence of noise.

Shell is a user interface for access to an operating system's services. In general, operating system shells use either a command-line interface (CLI) or graphical user interface (GUI), depending on a computer's role and particular operation.

Shock Rating is a rating (expressed in Gs) of how much shock a disk drive can sustain without damage. Operating and non-operating shock levels are usually specified separately.

Shouldering is a social engineering technique used to harvest passwords, PIN numbers and other sensitive data by discretely looking over someone's shoulder while they enter the information.

SIF standard Interchange Format and is a format for exchanging video images of 240 lines with 352 pixels each for NTSC, and 288 lines by 352 pixels for PAL and SECAM. At the nominal field rates of 60 and 50 fields/s, the two formats have the same data rate.

Sign Bit is usually the left most bit of a binary number used to indicate a positive(0) or negative (1) number.

Silicon Dioxide is grown on a wafer during chip fabrication to serve as an insulating layer.

Silicon Ingot is a large, cylindrical, single crystal made from purified silicon. The cylinder is sliced into thin wafers which are used for making computer chips.

Silicon Wafer is a slice of pure silicon used to fabricate integrated circuits such as microprocessors. The individual microcircuits are cut from the wafer using a process called wafer dicing. These microcircuits are then packaged as an integrated circuit.

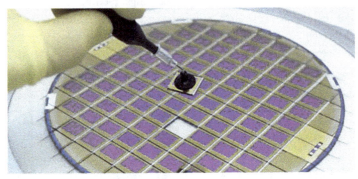

SIM stands for subscriber identity module and is an integrated circuit mounted on a small plastic card used to identify and authenticate subscribers on mobile devices.

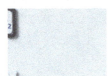

SIMM stands for Single In-Line Memory Module and typically come with a 32 data bit with a 72-pin connector that had to be installed in pairs to work properly. They were eventually replaced by the DIMMs.

Single Mode uses only one light ray (or mode) through a 9 micron cable and can transmit up to 100km.

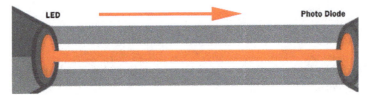

Sledgehammer is the codename for AMD's x86-64 design for extending the iA-32 architecture to support 64-bit code and memory addressing.

SLIP stands for Serial Line Internet Protocol and is a protocol that allows a computer to connect to the Internet through a connection and enjoy most of the benefits of a direct connection, including the ability to run graphical front ends such as Internet Browsers. SLIP is also used to run TCP/IP over phone lines. See also PPP.

Slot 1 is Intel's proprietary CPU interface form factor for Pentium II CPUs. Slot 1 replaces the Socket 7 and Socket 8 form factors used by previous Pentium processors. It is a 242-contact daughterboard slot that accepts a microprocessor packaged as a Single Edge Contact (SEC) cartridge. Communication between the Level 2 cache and CPU is at half the CPU's clock speed.

Slot 2 is an enhanced Slot 1, which uses a somewhat wider 330-way connector SEC cartridge that holds up to four processors. The biggest difference from Slot 1 is that the Level 2 runs at full processor speed.

Slot A is AMD's proprietary 242-way connector SEC cartridge used by their original Athlon processor. Physically identical to Slot 1 but electrically incompatible.

Slotted Mask is a variation on the aperture grill phosphor triad approach which uses the slot-mask design used on many non-Trinitron TV sets.

SmartMedia is an ultra-compact flash memory card format developed by Toshiba. Similar to an SD card, but slightly bigger and as thin as a credit card. SmartMedia cards were popular in early digital cameras around 2001 and could hold up to 128MB but were superseded by XD and SD cards.

SMDS stands for Switched Multimegabit Data Service and is a high-speed, switched data communications service offered by telephone companies for interconnecting separate local area networks (LANs) into a single wide area network (WAN). Prior to SMDS's arrival in 1995, the only way to connect LANs was through a dedicated private line. SMDS is becoming an increasingly attractive alternative because it is more flexible and usually more economical.

SMP stands for Symmetric Multiprocessing and is a computer architecture that provides fast performance by making multiple CPUs available to complete individual processes simultaneously (multiprocessing). Unlike asymmetrical processing, any idle processor can be assigned any task, and additional CPUs can be added to improve performance and handle increased loads.

SMPTE Timecode is an 80-bit standardised edit time code adopted by SMPTE, the Society of Motion Picture and Television Engineers. See also Time Code, for measuring video duration. Each frame is identified in the form hours:minutes:seconds:frames.

SMTP stands for Simple Mail Transport Protocol and is the protocol used to send e-mail on the internet.

SNA stands for Systems Network Architecture and is a mainframe network topology introduced by IBM in 1974. Originally designed as a centralised architecture with a host computer controlling many terminals, SNA has evolved over the years so that it now also supports peer-to-peer networks of workstations. SNA incorporates data protocols, network interface cards and just about every facet of communication.

SNR short for Signal-to-Noise Ratio and is a measure of link performance arrived at by dividing signal power by noise power. Typically measured in decibels. The higher the ratio, the clearer the connection.

Socket 370 is Intel's proprietary CPU interface form factor first introduced for its Celeron line of CPUs and subsequently adopted for later versions of the Pentium III family.

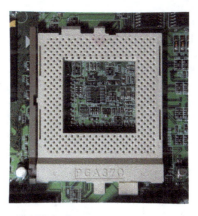

Socket 423 is Intel's proprietary CPU interface form factor used by its early Pentium 4 processors.

Socket 478 is Intel's proprietary CPU interface form factor which replaced Socket 423 with the advent of the 0.13-micron Pentium 4 Northwood core.

Socket 7 is the CPU interface form factor for fifth-generation Pentium-class CPU chips from Intel, Cyrix, and AMD.

Socket 754 is AMD's 754-pin CPU interface form factor introduced with its 64-bit Athlon 64 processor in the autumn of 2003.

Socket 8 is Intel's proprietary CPU interface form factor used exclusively by their sixth-generation Pentium Pro CPU chip. Socket 8 is a 387-pin ZIF socket with connections for the CPU and one or two SRAM dies for the Level 2 cache.

Socket A is AMD's 462-pin CPU interface form factor which replaced Slot A at the time of the introduction of the Thunderbird and Spitfire cores used by AMD's Athlon and Duron desktop processor ranges respectively.

Soft Error is an error in data or a signal. It can be corrected using ECC. Usually caused by power fluctuations or noise spikes.

Soft-Sectored disks mark the beginning of each sector of data within a track by a magnetic pattern.

SOHO stands for Small Office/Home Office and refers to a small business or business-at-home user with 1-10 workers.

SOI stands for Silicon-On-Insulator and is a silicon wafer with a thin layer of oxide – into which integrated circuits are built – buried in it. SOI substrates achieve superior isolation between adjacent devices in CMOS devices.

SOJ stands for Small Outline J-Lead package and is a plastic surface mount package designed for memory chips with pins that look like the letter J.

Solid State Drive or SSD, is a mass storage device used to store data on a computer system using flash memory.

Sound Blaster is a family of sound cards developed by Creative Labs.

Sound Card also known as an audio card, is an internal expansion card that facilitates the input and output of audio signals to and from a computer, providing the audio for multimedia applications such as music, editing video or audio, presentations, games and video projection through a speaker or sound system.

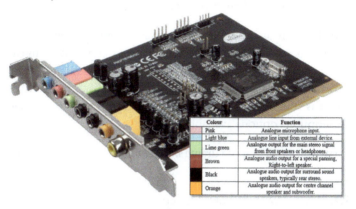

Colour	Function
Pink	Analogue microphone input.
Light blue	Analogue line input from external device.
Lime green	Analogue output for the main stereo signal from front speakers or headphones.
Brown	Analogue audio output for a special panning, Right-to-left speaker.
Black	Analogue audio output for surround sound speakers, typically rear stereo.
Orange	Analogue audio output for centre channel speaker and subwoofer.

South Bridge connects the CPU to the slower devices such as USB ports, hard drives, external drives, printers wifi/network cards, and other peripherals.

Spam is irrelevant or unsolicited messages sent over the Internet, typically to a large number of users, for the purposes of advertising, phishing, spreading malware, etc.

Specular Highlights are lighting characteristic that determines how light should reflect off an object. Specular highlights are typically white and can move around an object based on camera position.

Spindle is a disk drive's centre shaft on which the disk platters are mounted.

Spindle Speed is the velocity at which the disk media spins within a hard disk, measured in rpm (revolutions per minute). By the late 1990s EIDE hard disks generally features a 5,400rpm or 7,200 mechanism, while SCSI drives were usually either 7,200rpm or 10,000rpm.

Spline is a 3D bezier curve used in modelling.

Spline-Based Modelling is representing 3-D objects as surfaces made up of mathematically derived curves (splines).

Spotify is an audio streaming service where you can stream music and other content free. Spotify offers copyrighted music and podcasts, including more than 60 million songs, from record labels and media companies. Since the basic features are free it is funded with advertisements. However there are paid subscriptions options available .

Sprite is a small graphic drawn independently of the rest of the screen.

SQL short for Structured Query Language and is a query language developed by IBM that uses simple English language statements to perform database queries and operations.

```
SELECT * FROM Customers WHERE CustomerName
= "Alfred";
```

In the above statement "customers" is a table and "customername" is a field in that table. The statement would return.

CustomerID	CustomerName	Address
1	Alfred	303 Jumbony Road

SQL Injection is a code injection technique used to attack data-driven applications, in which nefarious SQL statements are inserted into an entry field for execution (e.g., to dump the database contents to the attacker).

SRAM stands for Static Random Access Memory and is a form of RAM that retains its data without the constant refreshing that DRAM requires. SRAM is generally used for caches as it offers faster memory access times, but it is also more expensive to manufacture.

S-Register is the RAM in a modem that is used to store the current configuration profile.

sRGB stands for Standardised Red, Green and Blue and is the colour space standard established by the International Electrotechnical Commission which forms the basis of colour matching hardware devices such as LCD monitors, projectors, printers, scanners, digital cameras and various applications, including the World Wide Web.

SSA stands for Serial Storage Architecture and is a peripheral interface from IBM whose ring configuration allows remaining devices to function if one fails. SCSI software can be mapped over SSA allowing existing SCSI devices to be used.

SSD see Solid Sate Drive.

SSE stands for Streaming SIMD Extensions and is Intel's SSE and SSE2 technologies are effectively sets of instructions for accelerating multimedia applications. SSE is found on Intel Pentium III processors; SSE2 is an incremental supported on Intel Pentium 4 processors. Some of the benefits of SSE/SSE2 include rendering higher quality images, high quality audio, MPEG2 video, simultaneous MPEG2 encoding and decoding and reduced CPU utilisation for speech recognition. See also SIMD.

SSH stands for Stands for Secure Shell and is a protocol for secure remote login to another machine. This provides a command prompt where you can issue commands to execute programs or perform tasks on the remote machine.

In Windows 10 and 11, you can connect using a program called PuTTY. You can also connect from the terminal or command prompt using the SSH command.

SSID stands for **S**ervice **S**et **ID**entifier and is the name of a WiFi network. A wireless router or access point broadcasts a SSID, allowing nearby devices to display a list of available networks.

SSL is short for Secure Sockets Layer and is a protocol used for encrypting an internet connection thereby safeguarding any data that is being sent or received. SSL uses asymmetrical cryptography which requires two cryptographic keys - one public known to everyone, one private only known by sender & receiver. You use the public key to encrypt the data, then the recipient uses the private key to decrypt it. Replaced by TLS.

ST506 introduced in 1979, Seagate's ST506 was the first hard disk drive for personal computers. Supporting 5.25in full-height drives with a capacity of between 5MB and 40MB, the ST506 interface became an industry standard for the IBM PC and its successors, eventually being superseded by the IDE interface.

Start Menu is a user interface element included in Microsoft Windows since Windows 95. It provides a central launching point for apps and other tasks. Accessed by clicking the Start button located on the taskbar. The Start Menu contains links to settings, recently used files, and apps.

Start/Stop Bits are the bits at the beginning and end of a data block when using asynchronous data transmission.

STP stands for Shielded Twisted Pair and is a telephone wire that is wrapped in a metal sheath to eliminate external interference.

String is a sequence of characters, typically used to represent text, which can include letters, numbers, symbols, and whitespace.

Streaming is a delivery method for transmitting data that is processed as a steady and continuous stream. Streaming allows the user to play media from the Internet without having to download the entire file first. Streaming has become popular thanks to high speed internet with many companies such as Netflix, Amazon Prime, and Apple offering on demand TV shows and films.

Subnetting is the practice of dividing a network into two or more networks. It is used to improve performance and enhance security by limiting the broadcast domain and minimizing network traffic.

Subnet Mask on a TCP/IP network, is the value used to separate the IP address of a device into two parts: the network ID and the device ID. For example the IP address

`192.168.1.6`

With a subnet mask of

`255.255.255.0`

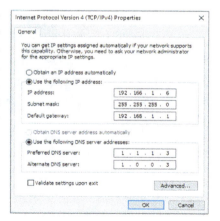

This means that 192.168.1 is the network ID, and 6 is the device ID. This allows you to divide up large networks into smaller networks called subnets.

Sub-sampling is a bandwidth reduction technique which reduces the amount of digital data used to represent an image. Part of a compression process.

Substrate is the underlying material on which a microelectronic device or storage media is built. Silicon is the most widely used substrate for chips, fibreglass for printed circuit boards and ceramic for multichip modules. Aluminium is commonly used for hard disks, glass for optical disks and mylar for floppy disks.

Subtractive colour is created when white light is reflected off a surface that doesn't produce its own light. The surface absorbs some colours (subtracting) and reflects the remaining, thereby creating a colour. A white surface reflects all the colours, a black surface absorbs all the colours. This colour scheme is commonly used in the print industry and is known as CMYK.

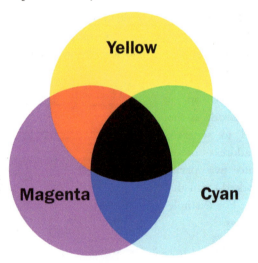

Supercomputer is a computer with a high level of performance as compared to a general-purpose computer. The performance of a supercomputer is commonly measured in floating-point operations per second (FLOPS) instead of million instructions per second (MIPS).

Superscalar is a CPU architecture that allows more than one instruction to be executed in one clock cycle. Processors can do this by fetching multiple instructions in one cycle, deciding which instructions are independent of other instructions, and executing them.

Surface is the top or bottom side of the platter that is coated with the magnetic material for recording data. On some drives one surface may be reserved for positioning information.

Sustained Transfer Rate is the amount of data a drive can continuously read or write per second.

SVCD or Super VCD is an evolution of the VCD format that uses MPEG-2 compression to store between 35 and 80 minutes (depending on bit rate) of SVHS quality video on a CD. Also known as Chaoji VCD.

SVGA stands for Super VGA and is a video display standard capable of handling a resolution of 800×600 256 colours, or 1024×768 16-colour support. The term was subsequently used to mean a resolution of 800×600 or greater, regardless of the number of colours available.

S-Video somewhat obsolete nowadays but was a video hardware standard used in Hi8, S-VHS video formats. It transmits luminance and colour portions separately,  using multiple wires, and avoids composite video encoding which can result in loss of picture quality. Also known as Y-C Video.

Swap Space is a dedicated portion of a storage device used by the operating system as temporary memory when physical RAM is full. It helps maintain system performance by allowing inactive pages to be moved from RAM to disk storage, though it is significantly slower than RAM..

Switch is a network device that operates at the data link layer (Layer 2) of the OSI reference model and whose fu
nction is to forward packets of data according to their destination address. A switch maintains a table of MAC addresses of each device connected and what port it's physically plugged into. This means the switch can forward a packet only to the port the device is connected to rather than to every port on the switch, thereby making the full bandwidth available each sender and receiver.

Switched Ethernet is an Ethernet network that is constructed using switches.

SXGA or super XGA is a screen resolution of 1280×1024 pixels, regardless of the number of colours available.

Synchronous refers to any events that are synchronised, or co-ordinated by a regular clock pulse. Communication within a computer is usually synchronous and is governed by the microprocessor clock. Signals along the bus, for example, can occur only at specific points in the clock cycle.

Synchronous Cache is a type of high-speed memory that operates in sync with the system clock, reducing access delays and improving data transfer rates between the processor and main memory. It is commonly used in Level 2 (L2) and Level 3 (L3) CPU caches.

Syntax Error is an error in the syntax of a sequence of characters or tokens that is intended to be written in a particular programming language.

Syntax Highlighting is a feature in many text editors that displays source code in different colors and fonts according to the category of terms. This feature facilitates a more comfortable reading of the source code.

System Bus is the primary pathway between the CPU, memory and high-speed peripherals to which expansion buses, such as ISA, EISA, PCI and VL-Bus, can connect. Also referred to as the external bus or host bus, and came to be used interchangeably with frontside bus (FSB) following the introduction of Intel's Dual Independent Bus (DIB) architecture in 1997.

System on a Chip (SOC) is is an integrated circuit (IC) that integrates all components of a computer or other electronic system into a single chip. It combines various computer components, including a central processing unit (CPU), memory, input/output ports, and often other features such as graphics processing units (GPU) and network connectivity, on a single substrate or microchip. SoCs are designed to offer a complete computing solution within a compact footprint, reducing power consumption and cost while increasing reliability and performance. They are widely used in mobile devices, embedded systems, and increasingly in more traditional computing environments.

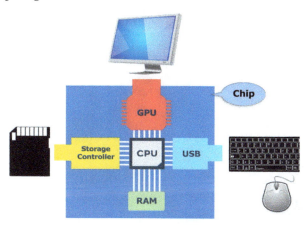

T

T&L stands for Transform and Lighting and is two separate engines on the GPU that provide for a powerful, balanced PC platform and enable extremely high polygon count scenes. Transform performance determines how complex objects can be and how many can appear in a scene without sacrificing frame rate. Lighting techniques add to a scene's realism by changing the appearance of objects based on light sources.

T1 a digital transmission standard in the U.S. and Canada that carries data at 1.544 Mbps and supports 24 voice or data channels. The European equivalent, E1, operates at 2.048 Mbps and carries 32 channels.

Tag is the subset of the CPU address bits used to compare the tag bits of the cache directory to the main memory address being accessed.

Tag RAM is a section of high-speed memory in a CPU cache that stores address tags, allowing the processor to quickly check whether a requested memory address is already in the cache without performing a full lookup in main memory.

TAPI stands for Telephony Application Programming Interface and is an API that allows windows applications to program telephone-line-based devices such as modems and fax machines in a device-independent manner.

Taskbar in Windows 10, is the bar that sits along the bottom of the screen and shows which apps are currently running. You'll also see the start button on the far left. And on the far right, system status icons, the clock and action center.

TB short for Terabyte, a unit of data storage equivalent to 1 trillion bytes. Tebibyte (TiB) is 1,099,511,627,776 bytes

TCP/IP stands for Transmission Control Protocol/Internet Protocol and is a suite of communication protocols devices use to communicate over the internet. The TCP/IP model, like the OSI model, uses a layered approach and has four layers.

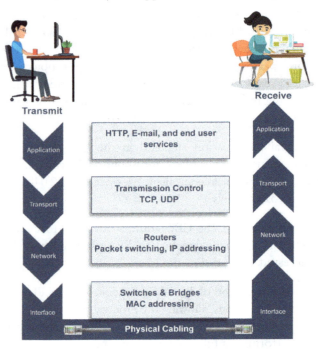

TDM stands for Time Division Multiplexing and is a data communications technique that interleaves separate data streams into one high-speed transmission by assigning each stream a different time slice in a set. The receiving end then divides the single stream back into its original constituent signals.

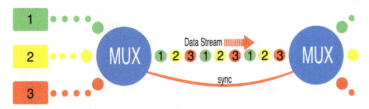

TDMA stands for Time Division Multiple Access and is a mobile communications technique in which a radio frequency channel is divided into time slots, each of which lasts for a fraction of a second. TDMA divides a 30KHz channel into six time slots that are allocated in pairs, resulting in three usable TDMA channels. Any given conversation can use one or more of every third time slot on an ongoing basis during a call.

Tearing is a video artefact in which portions of a video window are not updated in time for the next frame.

Teleconference is a general term for a meeting not held in person. Usually refers to a multi-party telephone call, set up by the phone company or private source, which enables more than two callers to participate in a conversation. The growing use of video allows participants at remote locations to see, hear, and participate in proceedings, or share visual data ("video conference").

Tesla Magnetic fields, or more specifically, magnetic flux densities historically have been measured with a unit called the milligauss – 1 milligauss(mg) being equal to 0.001 Gauss(g). Electrical engineers and physicists use the Tesla as a unit of international standard, one Tesla being the equivalent to 10,000 Gauss or 10,000,000 milligauss. Typically the Tesla is used in technical journals and the milligauss unit is used in information for the general public.

Tessellation is the process of dividing an object or surface into geometric primitives (triangles, quadrilaterals, or other polygons) for simplified processing and rendering.

Texel is a textured picture element. The basic unit of measurement when dealing with texture-mapped 3D objects.

Texture is a 2 dimensional bitmap pasted onto a 3D object or polygon to add realism.

Texture Filtering bilinear or trilinear filtering. Also known as sub texel positioning. If a pixel is in between texels, the program colours the pixel with an average of the texels' colours instead of assigning it the exact colour of one single texel. If this is not done, the texture gets very blocky up close as multiple pixels get the exact same texel colouring, while the texture shimmers at a distance because small position changes keep producing large texel changes.

Texture Mapping is the application of a bitmap image onto a 3D shape to create different surfaces. Texture maps can vary in size and detail, and can be pasted onto various different shapes such as cylinders, spheres, cubes and so on.

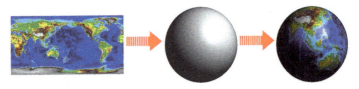

Texture Memory is used to store or buffer textures to be mapped on to 3D polygon objects.

TFT Stands for Thin Film Transistor, and is a type of LCD flat-panel display screen, in which each pixel is controlled by one to four transistors. TFT technology provides the best resolution of all the current flat-panel techniques. TFT screens are sometimes called active- matrix LCDs.

Thermal Recalibration is the periodic sensing of the temperature in hard disk drives so as to make minor adjustments to the alignment servo and data platters. In an AV drive, this process is performed only in idle periods so that there is no interruption in reading and writing long streams of digital video data.

Thermal Compound a paste often applied between a CPU and it's heatsink to ensure best possible contact and transfer of heat

Thermal Transfer is a printer technology that uses heat to transfer coloured dye onto paper.

Thermo Autochrome is a print technology used in digital camera companion printers that claimed to produce photographic quality output on a par with the more well-known dye sublimation printers.

Thin Film is a type of coating allowing very thin layers of magnetic material used on hard disks and read/write heads. Hard disks with thin film surfaces can store greater amounts of data.

Thread is the smallest executable unit of a process. A process can have multiple threads running as part of it.

Thunderbolt is a high-speed hardware interface developed by Intel in collaboration with Apple that combines data transfer, video output, audio, and power into a single connection. Thunderbolt 1 & 2 use Mini DisplayPort connectors, while Thunderbolt 3 & 4 use USB-C. Thunderbolt 3 & 4 support up to 40 Gbps transfer speeds and can daisy-chain multiple devices.

TiB short for Tebibyte and is a unit of storage consisting of is 1,099,511,627,776 bytes.

TIFF stands for Tagged Image File Format and is a popular file format for bitmapped graphics that stores the data in discrete blocks called tags. Each tag contains a particular attribute of the image, such as its width or height, the compression method used (if any), and a textual description of the image.

Time Code is a frame-by-frame address code time reference recorded on the spare track of a videotape or inserted in the vertical blanking interval. It is an eight-digit number encoding time in hours, minutes, seconds, and video frames (e.g.:02:04:48:26).

Time Line is a scale measured in either frames or seconds that provides an editable sequence of images, animation, and video clips to produce a final video. Here below, you can see a time line for an Adobe Premiere Video Project.

TLB short for Translation Lookaside Buffer and is a section of memory within a processor which caches part of the translation from virtual addresses to physical addresses. Also referred to as Address Translation Cache.

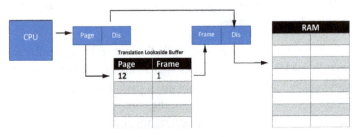

Token Ring is a local area network (LAN) technology developed by IBM (IEEE 802.5) where a special packet called a token is passed around the network ring. Only the PC with the token is allowed to send data onto the ring.

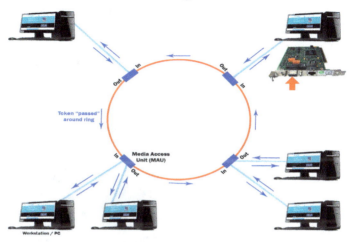

Tone Dialling is one of two methods of dialling the telephone. (The other is pulse dialling.) With tone dialling, the modem sends tones of different frequencies to represent the telephone numbers. Tone dialling is normally associated with push-button (touch-tone) phones and is also called Dual Tone Multi-Frequency (DTMF) dialling.

Toner is a fine powder used by copy machines and laser printers which consists of a dry, powdery substance that is attracted to an electrostatically charged drum, in order to create the image to be printed onto the paper.

TOR is short for The Onion Router, and is a privacy-focused network that anonymizes internet traffic by routing it through multiple encrypted relays (called nodes) before reaching its destination. While it obscures a user's origin and prevents tracking, traffic at the exit node is not encrypted, meaning unencrypted data can be intercepted.

When you use Tor to browse the internet, your data is wrapped in multiple layers of encryption and sent through a random pathway of relays (or nodes). Each relay peels away a single layer of encryption to reveal the location of the next relay in the circuit. This process ensures that no single relay knows both the original source and the final destination of the data. The final relay in this pathway, known as the exit node, removes the last layer of encryption and sends the data to its final destination.

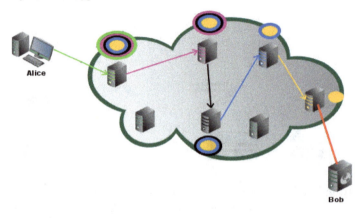

Tracert, a command line utility used to trace the route of a packet between various hosts on a network

Topology is the pattern of interconnection between nodes in a communications network.

Toslink is a fibre optic digital audio connection used to connect a digital source component (e.g., DVD player, CD player, etc.) to a receiver or pre-amplifier. By passing the "raw" digital audio signal using laser (light) pulses, interference and degradation are minimised. The means of interconnect used for connecting MiniDisc players to stereos and certain sound cards.

TPI stands for Tracks Per Inch and is the number of tracks written within each inch of a storage medium's recording surface.

TPM or Trusted Platform Module is a chip usually mounted on the motherboard that securely stores passwords, certificates, or encryption keys that are used to authenticate a PC or laptop so that malware can't access or tamper with that data

Track is a subdivision of the recording area of storage media, such as magnetic disks, optical discs and magnetic tape.

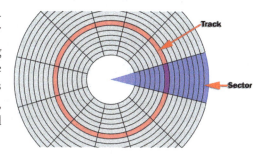

Transceiver a term used to describe a combination of transmitter and receiver. In the context of networking, a transceiver is an electronic interface or adapter between the Ethernet coaxial cable and the drop cable that attaches to network devices to provide the drive, reception, and collision detection between physical network media.

Transcoding is the process of converting audio, video, or other media files from one format to another. Transcoding is commonly used to make media playable on different devices or to reduce the file size for storage or streaming.

Transfer Rate is the rate at which the disk drive sends and receives data from the controller. The sustained transfer rate includes the time required for system processing, head switches, and seeks, and accurately reflects the drive's true performance. The burst mode transfer rate is a much higher figure that refers only to the movement of data directly into RAM.

Transistor is a device used to amplify a signal or open and close a circuit. In a computer, it functions as an electronic switch, or bridge. The transistor contains a semiconductor material that can change its electrical state when pulsed.

Transparency is the quality of being able to see through a material. The terms transparency and translucency are often used synonymously; however, transparent would technically mean "seeing through clear glass," while translucent would mean "seeing through frosted glass."

Trichromatic is the technical name for RGB representation of colour to create all the colours in the spectrum.

Trojan is the name and concept derived from the story of the Trojan horse used to invade the city of Troy. In computing, a trojan masquerades as an ordinary program or utility that carries a hidden, more sinister function. This could be data theft, or a ransomware attack.

True Black is produced using a separate black ink rather than a mixture of cyan, magenta and yellow. See also Composite Black.

True Colour is the ability to generate 16,777,216 colours (24-bit colour).

TrueType is a font standard developed by Apple and Microsoft in the late 1980s as a competitor to Adobe's Type 1 fonts used in PostScript. TrueType fonts are scalable fonts that can be resized to any size without losing quality.

TTL stands for Time To Live and is a mechanism that limits the lifespan or the number of hops a data packet is allowed to take through a network before being discarded. It is used to prevent data packets from circulating indefinitely in case of a routing loop. Each time a packet passes through a router, the router decreases the packet's TTL value by one. In DNS, TTL determines how long a record is cached before requiring an update.

TWAIN is an interface that enables an application to communicate with a scanner or other image capture device.

Tweening also known as in-betweening is calculating the intermediate frames between two keyframes to simulate smooth motion.

Twisted Pair is a type of cabling in which two insulated copper wires are twisted together to reduce electromagnetic interference known as crosstalk. It is commonly used in Ethernet networks (Cat5e, Cat6, Cat7) and ISDN lines to carry voice and data signals.

Two's Complement is a binary number system that encodes positive and negative integers. The bit on the left is known as the most significant bit or MSB and is used to indicate a positive (0) or negative (1) number.

Sign	4	2	1
1	1	0	1

The remaining bits are used to store the value itself.

Decimal	Two's-complement
4	0100
3	0011
2	0010
1	0001
0	0000
-1	1111
-2	1110
-3	1101
-4	1100

To convert a binary number to two's complement, invert each bit. Add 1 to the rightmost bit (least significant bit).

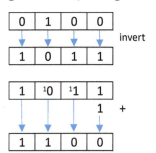

Two-Factor Authentication is an authentication method that requires a user to verify their identity using two different methods before gaining access to an account. This can be a phone text message, email message, biometric verification, or some authenticator app.

Typeface is a family of characters what have a similar design, eg, Times New Roman. See font.

U

UART stands for Universal Asynchronous Receiver Transmitter and is the chip that drives a serial port.

Ubuntu Linux is a popular open-source operating system based on the Linux kernel and the Debian distribution. It is known for its user-friendly interface, stability, and extensive community support.

UEFI stands for Unified Extensible Firmware Interface and is a modern firmware interface for computers, designed to replace the older BIOS (Basic Input/Output System) firmware interface. UEFI provides a standardized, high-level interface between the operating system and the firmware, offering features such as graphical menus, remote diagnostics and repair over networks, secure boot to protect against malware attacking the boot process, and support for GPT drives larger than 2 terabytes. It facilitates faster boot and shutdown times as well as enhanced security features compared to the legacy BIOS systems.

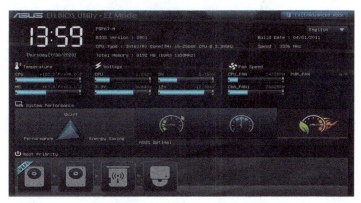

ULSI stands for Ultra Large Scale Integration and is a chip with more than one million transistors.

Ultra DMA is a data transfer protocol used in ATA (IDE) hard drives that improved transfer speeds by allowing direct memory access without relying heavily on the CPU.

UMTS short for Universal Mobile Telecommunications System, is a third-generation (3G) mobile telecommunications technology that provides high-speed data and voice services to mobile devices. Developed as an evolution of the Global System for Mobile Communications (GSM).

UNC stands for Universal Naming Convention and is a standard used to locate a shared resource on a local area network. On a windows network:

```
\\server-name\shared-resource
```

On a unix/linux network

```
//server-name/shared-resource
```

Unformatted Capacity is the total number of usable bytes on a disk, including the space that will be required later to record location, boundary definitions, and timing information. See also formatted capacity.

Unicode is a standardized character encoding system that assigns a unique numerical value (code point) to every character in the world's writing systems, including alphabets, ideographs, symbols, and emoji. It allows computers to represent and manipulate text from different languages and scripts using a single, universal character set. Unicode supports over 143,000 characters, with each character assigned a unique code point ranging from U+0000 to U+10FFFF in hexadecimal notation. This ensures consistency and interoperability across different platforms, applications, and languages, enabling seamless communication and text processing on a global scale. Unicode encoding schemes, such as UTF-8, UTF-16, and UTF-32, specify how these code points are represented as binary data for storage and transmission in computer systems.

Unix is a multi-user, multi-tasking operating system originally developed by Ken Thompson at AT&T Bell Labs in the late 1960s and early 70s. The core of Unix is the kernel which allocates CPU time and memory to programs, handles devices and the file system. When using Unix, you interact with the operating system using a shell - a user interface where you can type in commands.

URL is short for Uniform Resource Locator (or Location) and describes the address of a website. For example:

www.elluminetpress.com

The URL itself can be broken down into its basic elements. Lets take a closer look at an example.

- **www** means the server hosting the service, in this case www for World Wide Web. Usually points to your public_html directory on the web server.
- **elluminetpress** is the domain name or organisation's name and is unique to that organisation.
- **.com** is the type of site. It can be .co.x for country specific companies (eg .co.uk), .org for no profit organisations, or .gov for government organisations. These are known as top level domain names and are designed to identify the types of companies represented on the web.

USB, short for Universal Serial Bus, is a widely-used industry standard for connecting peripherals and external devices to computers and other electronic devices. It provides a standardized interface for data transfer, power supply, and communication between devices. USB ports are found on most computers, laptops, tablets, smartphones, and other consumer electronics devices. USB has evolved over the years with different versions and standards, including USB 1.x, USB 2.0, USB 3.x, and USB4, each offering improvements in data transfer speeds, power delivery, and compatibility.

USB 2.0 transfers data at a maximum rate of approximately 480 Mbps, equivalent to around 60 Megabytes per second. USB 2.0 ports and connectors are typically colored black.

USB 3.0 (USB 3.1 Gen 1), also known as SuperSpeed USB, offers significantly faster data transfer speeds, reaching up to 5 Gbps, or about 640 Megabytes per second. These higher speeds make USB 3.0 ideal for demanding applications such as external hard drives and high-speed devices. USB 3.0 ports and connectors are often distinguishable by their blue color. Later rebranded as USB 3.1 Gen 1

USB 3.1 Gen 2 doubled this speed to 10 Gbps, while USB 3.2 further enhanced efficiency and introduced a new 20 Gbps speed tier. These iterations of USB 3.x provide increasingly faster data transfer rates, making them ideal for various high-speed applications such as external storage devices, gaming peripherals, and multimedia equipment.

USB 3.2 further advanced the standard by introducing multi-lane operation, effectively doubling the bandwidth again to 20 Gbps when using compatible cables and devices.

USB C short for USB Type-C, is a 24-pin USB connector system characterized by a reversible, flippable design and a compact shape.

It represents a significant improvement over previous USB connectors due to its ability to support a variety of protocols using the "Alternate Mode" feature. With USB-C, devices can utilize the same port and cable for multiple purposes, including data transfer, charging, and video output. USB-C supports USB standards up to USB4, offering data transfer rates that can reach up to 40 Gbps depending on the USB version implemented. It is widely adopted across a broad range of devices, including smartphones, tablets, laptops, and peripherals, for its versatility and ease of use. USB-C also supports the USB Power Delivery (USB PD) specification, which allows for faster charging and the delivery of up to 100 watts of power, enabling devices like laptops to be charged through the same port used for data transfer.

USB Drive is an external data storage device such as a portable hard disk drive, or a flash drive that can be plugged into a USB port.

USB Stick, or flash drive, is a data storage device that uses flash memory to store data and can be plugged into a USB port.

USB-IF stands for USB Implementers Forum and is a non-profit corporation founded by the group of companies that developed the Universal Serial Bus specification to provide a support organization and forum for the advancement and adoption of USB technology. The Forum facilitates the development of high-quality compatible USB peripherals (devices), and promotes the benefits of USB and the quality of products that have passed compliance testing.

UTF-8 is a variable-width character encoding standard that is widely used for representing Unicode characters. It can represent every character in the Unicode character set using one to four bytes. In UTF-8, ASCII characters (0-127) are represented using a single byte, ensuring compatibility with ASCII-encoded text. Characters beyond the ASCII range are represented using multiple bytes, with the number of bytes depending on the Unicode code point. UTF-8 encoding is efficient for storing and transmitting text, especially for English and other Western languages where most characters fit within the ASCII range. It is also backward compatible with ASCII and supports multilingual text, making it one of the most commonly used encoding standards on the web.UTF-8 is backwards compatible with ASCII and widely used in internet web pages. In your HTML code you might see something like this: `<meta charset="utf-8">`. See unicode.

300

UTF-16 is a variable-width character encoding standard used for representing Unicode characters. It uses either two or four bytes to represent each character in the Unicode character set. Characters within the Basic Multilingual Plane (BMP), which includes most commonly used characters, are represented using two bytes, while characters outside the BMP are represented using four bytes. UTF-16 encoding is commonly used in programming languages like Java and JavaScript, as well as in Microsoft Windows operating systems. However, it may require additional memory and storage compared to UTF-8 for languages predominantly using characters within the BMP.

UTF-32 is a fixed-width Unicode encoding scheme that uses four bytes (32 bits) for every character, regardless of its Unicode code point. Unlike UTF-8 and UTF-16, which use variable-length encoding, UTF-32 simplifies text processing by ensuring each character is represented by a fixed number of bytes. However, it is less memory efficient than UTF-8 or UTF-16, as it always uses four bytes per character, even for common characters that could be stored in fewer bytes using other encodings. UTF-32 is primarily used in specialized applications where uniform character width is needed, such as certain programming environments and text processing systems.

UTP short for Unshielded Twisted-Pair, and is a type of copper cabling used in networking and telecommunications. It consists of pairs of insulated copper wires twisted together to minimize electromagnetic interference (EMI) and crosstalk. UTP is widely used  in Ethernet networks (eCat5e, Cat6, Cat6a), telephone systems, and other data communication applications. Its flexibility, cost-effectiveness, and ease of installation make it the most common choice for wired network infrastructure.

UTRAN stands for UMTS Terrestrial Radio Access Network and is the name of the WCDMA radio network in UMTS.

UV Light or Ultraviolet Light has a very short wavelengths and is just beyond the violet end of the visible spectrum. It is used to expose patterns on the layers of the microprocessor in a process much like photography.

UXGA stands for Ultra XGA and is a screen resolution of 1600×1200 pixels.

V

V.34 is an ITU modem standard for data transmission at up to 33.6 Kbit/s. V.34 is the successor to several earlier ITU standards, and most V.34 modems can interoperate with older, slower modems.

V.90 is an ITU-T modem standard, officially approved on February 4, 1998, which ended the competition between two rival 56 Kbit/s technologies: X2 and K56Flex. V.90 enabled downstream speeds of up to 56 Kbit/s and upstream speeds of up to 33.6 Kbit/s. It was later succeeded by the V.92 standard.

VAR stands for Value Added Reseller and is a company which resells hardware and software packages to developers and end users.

VBR stands for Variable Bit Rate and varies the amount of data per segment allowing a higher bit rate for more complex segments, such as more action or movement in a video, and a lower bit rate for less complex segments.

VCR stands for Video Cassette Recorder and is a videotape recording and playback machine that is available in several formats. Sony's Beta tape was the first VCR format, but is now defunct in favour of VHS which became the most commonly used format.

VDI or Virtual Desktop Infrastructure, is a technology that hosts desktop environments on a centralized server and allows users to access their desktops remotely over a network. Instead of running an operating system locally on a device, VDI delivers a virtualized desktop that users can interact with as if it were running on their own machine.

VDRV stands for Variable Data Rate Video and in digital systems, the ability to vary the amount of data processed per frame to match image quality and transmission bandwidth requirements. DVI symmetrical and asymmetrical systems can compress video at variable data rates.

VDSL is a high-speed broadband technology that provides faster data transmission over copper telephone over short distances (such as 1km). It is often used in FTTC networks.

Vector Graphics are a type of digital image composed of paths defined by mathematical equations, rather than pixels. These paths consist of points, lines, curves, and shapes, allowing vector graphics to be scaled infinitely without losing quality. Commonly used in logos, illustrations, and CAD designs. Vector graphics can be created using Adobe Illustrator and saved as SVG, AI, and EPS.

Vertex is a dimensionless position in three or four-dimensional space at which two or more lines (for instance, edges) intersect.

VESA stands for Video Electronics Standards Association and is an international non-profit organisation established in 1989 to set and support industry-wide interface standards designed for the PC, workstation, and other computing environments. The VESA Local Bus (VL-Bus) standard – introduced in 1992 and widely used before the advent of PCI – was a 32-bit local bus standard compatible with both ISA and EISA cards.

VFAT stands for Virtual File Allocation Table and is an extension of the FAT (File Allocation Table) file system, introduced in Windows 95 to support long filenames (LFN) while maintaining compatibility with older 16-bit FAT16 systems.

VfW stands for Video for Windows and is a standard established by Microsoft for the integration of digital video, animation and sound which uses the .AVI file format. The necessary software drivers are incorporated into the Windows operating system.

VGA also referred to as Video Graphics Adapter (or Array), is a display standard introduced by IBM in 1987 for its PS/2 computers. It quickly became the foundation for most PC graphics and remains widely supported. The original VGA standard provides a resolution of 640×480 pixels with 16 colors or 320×200 pixels with 256 colors in graphics mode. VGA also introduced analog video signaling, making it compatible with CRT monitors and later LCDs via VGA connectors. Over time, VGA has been succeeded by higher-resolution standards like SVGA, XGA, and HDMI, but the 15-pin VGA connector remains in use for legacy support in some displays and projectors..

VGA Feature Connector is a standard 26-pin plug for passing the VGA signal on to some other device, often a video overlay board. This feature connector cannot pass the high-resolution signal from the card and is limited to VGA.

VHS or Video Home System, is an analog video recording format developed by JVC in 1976. It became the dominant home video format in the late 20th century, replacing competing format Betamax due to its longer recording time, lower cost, and widespread adoption by movie studios.

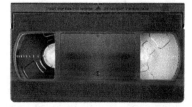

VidCap is Microsoft's Video For Windows program to capture video input to RAM or hard disk memory.

Video Capture is performed by an expansion card that digitises full motion video from a VCR, camera or other video source. The digital video is then stored in a compressed format on hard disk.

Video Card or graphics card is responsible for processing video, graphic and visual effects you see on your monitor. The graphics card is also known as a GPU (graphics processing unit).

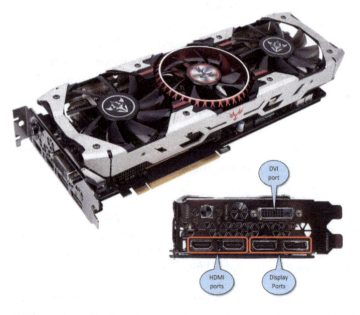

Video Mapping is a feature allowing the mapping of an AVI, MPEG movie or animation on to the surface of a 3D object.

Video Memory is the RAM built onto the graphics card used for processing graphics.

Video Scaling and Interpolation When scaled upwards, video clips tend to become pixelated, resulting in block image.

Hardware scaling and interpolation routines smooth out these jagged artefacts to create a more realistic picture. Better interpolation routines work on both the X and Y axis to prevent stepping on curved and diagonal elements.

Video1 is the default video compression algorithm in Microsoft's Video for Windows. Can produce 8- or 16-bit video sequences.

VideoCD is a format that allows the viewing of MPEG-1 (also known as the ISO IEC 11172 compression standard) video on CD-ROM. Originally devised by Philips, it allows for more than an hour of compressed video, the audio also being compressed and giving hi-fi standard. The whole point of VideoCD is cross-platform compatibility. The discs should work on suitably equipped PCs, Macs, dedicated VideoCD players, and CD-i systems. Video CD is based on the White Book standard developed by Philips and other industry leaders. Also referred to as VCD.

Virtual Desktop is a feature of many modern desktop operating systems such as MacOS and Windows 10 that allows you to create multiple, separate desktops where each can display different windows and apps.

Virtual Reality or VR is a system that allows the user to experience an immersive interaction with a computer generated 3D world. Some VR systems incorporate special headsets, visors, and gloves to simulate the environment.

Virtual Machine is a software-based emulation of a physical computer that runs an operating system and applications just like a physical machine. A VM operates within a host system using virtualized resources such as CPU, memory, and storage. It allows multiple operating systems to run on a single hardware platform independently. Examples include VMware Workstation, Microsoft Hyper-V, Oracle VirtualBox.

Virtual Memory an allocated portion of a computers hard disk drive or secondary storage used as if it were main memory (RAM).

Virus is a type of malware that replicates by attaching itself to other programs or files. Often requiring user action (such as opening an infected file) to spread.

Viterbi Decoder is a decoding algorithm developed in the late 1960s by Andrew Viterbi and used to decode a particular convolutional code (i.e. that adds redundancy to the data to improve the signal-to-noise ratio). Viterbi decoders output a 0 or a 1 based on an estimate of the input signal. Viterbi decoders are needed for reading HD DVD and Blu-ray discs.

VLB stands for VESA Local Bus or VL-Bus: the 32-bit local-bus standard created by the Video Electronics Standards Association (VESA) to provide a fast data connection between CPUs and local-bus devices. The VL-Bus was widely used in 486 PCs, but has since been replaced by the Intel PCI Bus.

VLSI stands for Very Large Scale Integration and is the process of placing hundreds of thousands (between 100,000 and one million) of electronic components on a single chip. Nearly all modern chips employ VLSI architectures, or ULSI (ultra large scale integration).

VM Channel stands for Vesa Media Channel, VESA's video bus which avoids the main system bus.

Voice Coil is a fast and reliable actuator that works like a loudspeaker, with the force of a magnetic coil causing a proportionate movement of the head.

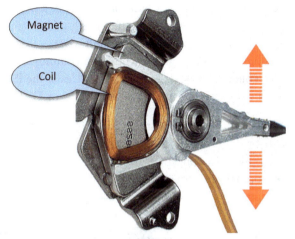

Voice coils are used to move the actuator arm on a hard disk drive and are more durable than stepper counterparts since they provide higher performance.

Voice recognition is the conversion of spoken words into computer text. Speech is first digitised and then matched against a dictionary of coded waveforms. The matches are then converted into text as if the words were typed on the keyboard.

VoIP stands for Voice over IP and is the technology used to transmit voice conversations over a data network using the Internet Protocol. The data network involved might be the Internet itself, or a corporate intranet, or managed networks used by local or long distance carriers and ISPs. An example of the later would be sip trunking. The technique promises drastically reduced costs to carriers and therefore prices to end users. Also referred to as IP Telephony.

Volatile Memory is memory that loses its contents when the power is turned off. A computer's main memory, made up of dynamic RAM or static RAM chips, loses its content immediately upon loss of power. Contrast ROM, which is non-volatile memory.

Volume in the context of a hard disk drive, is a storage area usually on a partition that is formatted using a file system such as FAT or NTFS. In windows, a volume is allocated a drive letter. A single hard disk can have multiple volumes and, unlike partitions, volumes can span multiple disks. Under the ISO 9660 standard, a volume refers to a single CD-ROM or DVD disk.

Von Neumann Architecture is a computer architecture described by John Von Neumann in 1940s which introduced the stored-program concept, where program instructions and data are stored in the same memory.

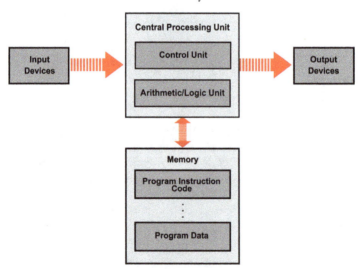

Instructions are fetched from memory sequentially and executed by the processor. Any data required by the program is fetched from memory, and any result from the execution is stored back in memory.

A processor based on Von Neumann architecture has several registers used during execution of an instruction, these are:

- Memory Address Register (MAR)
- Memory Data Register (MDR)
- Current Instruction Register (CIR)
- Program Counter (PC)
- Accumulator (ACC)

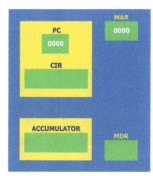

The registers and key elements of the Von Neumann architecture are used during the fetch-decode-execute cycle.

VPN stands for Virtual Private Network is a technology that creates a secure, encrypted connection over a public network, such as the Internet, to protect data and maintain privacy. It uses tunneling protocols and security procedures to ensure that transmitted information remains confidential. VPNs are often used to provide secure remote access, protect online privacy, and bypass geographical restrictions.

VRAM is a specialized type of memory used in graphics cards to store image and video data for rapid access by the GPU. VRAM enables smooth rendering of graphics, textures, and video by providing high-speed buffering for display output. Unlike standard RAM, VRAM is optimized for simultaneous reading and writing operations, ensuring efficient processing of high-resolution visuals and complex 3D graphics. Common types include GDDR VRAM, such as GDDR5, and GDDR6.

VRM stands for Voltage Regulator Module and is used to absorb the voltage difference between a CPU which may be added in the future and the motherboard.

VRML stands for Virtual Reality Modelling Language and is a database description language applied to create 3D worlds. VRML viewers, similar to HTML Web browsers, interpret VRML data downloaded from the Web and render it on your computer. This allows the bulk of the processing to be performed locally, and drastically reduces the volume of information for transmittal from the Web. Has since been since been replaced by WebGL.

VUMA stands for VESA Unified Memory Architecture and is a standard which establishes the electrical and logical interface between a system controller and an external VUMA device enabling them to share physical system memory.

VXD or virtual device driver. A type of device driver used in older Microsoft Windows operating systems (primarily Windows 3.x and Windows 9x) to manage hardware and system resources in a virtualized environment. VxDs operate in kernel mode, allowing direct access to hardware and system memory while enabling multiple applications to share system resources efficiently. They were eventually replaced by WDM (Windows Driver Model) in later Windows versions, which provided better stability and compatibility across different Windows operating systems.

W

Wafer Fab also known as a semiconductor fabrication plant is where all of a semiconductor's electronic components are interconnected onto a single die of silicon.

WAN stands for Wide Area Network and is a geographically dispersed network formed by linking several computers or local area networks (LANs) together over long distances, usually using leased long-distance lines. WANs can connect systems across town, in different cities, or in different regions of the world.

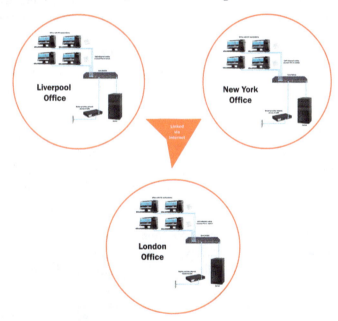

WAP stands for Wireless Application Protocol and is a protocol that enables Internet services to be delivered to small-screen mobile devices. The application via which WAP-enabled devices access Web content is referred to as a "micro-browser".

313

Watermark is typically a faint or transparent mark added to an image, document, or video for copyright protection, branding, or authenticity verification. It is not always decorative

WAV is a standard digital audio file format developed by Microsoft and IBM for storing uncompressed audio on Windows systems. WAV files typically contain high-quality, lossless audio data, supporting various bit depths (e.g., 8-bit, 16-bit, 24-bit, 32-bit) and sample rates (e.g., 44.1kHz, 48kHz, 96kHz). While commonly used for professional audio recording and editing, WAV files can also store compressed audio using codecs such as ADPCM. The file extension for this format is .wav.

WaveTable Synthesis is a common method for generating sound electronically on a PC. Output is produced using a table of sound samples -actual recorded sounds – that are digitised and played back as needed. By continuously rereading samples and looping them together at different pitches, highly complex tones can be generated from a minimum of stored data without overtaxing the processor.

WCDMA stands for Wideband Code Division Multiple Access and is a 3G wideband radio technique which makes highly efficient use of radio spectrum and is capable of supporting data rates of up to 2 Mbit/s, sufficient to allow simultaneous access to several voice, video and data services at once.

Web Browser is a client application that fetches and displays Web pages and other WWW resources to the user. The most popular browsers are Microsoft's Edge, Google Chrome and Firefox.

WEP is a security protocol for securing a Wi-Fi network. It was part of the original IEEE 802.11 standard ratified in 1997 but is now considered outdated and insecure due to its vulnerabilities to hacking.

Widget in software development is a component of a user interface that displays information or provides a way for a user to interact with the application, eg a button, drop down box, tab, dialog box or text field. In the context of operating systems (windows, mac, android, iOS, etc), a widget is a small software application or component that provides easy access to frequently used functions or to display information such as news, weather, calendar or a clock.

Wi-Fi is a wireless networking technology that enables devices such as computers, smartphones, and other equipment to communicate over a wireless signal. Utilizing  radio waves, Wi-Fi facilitates high-speed Internet and network connections without necessitating physical connections through cables. Governed by the IEEE 802.11 family of standards, Wi-Fi networks are prevalent in homes, businesses, and public areas, providing Internet access within the vicinity of a wireless access point. To ensure the security of transmitted data, Wi-Fi networks can employ encryption protocols like WPA, WPA2, and the latest WPA3. The technology supports multiple frequencies, notably the 2.4 GHz and 5 GHz bands, each offering distinct ranges and performance characteristics to suit a range of networking requirements. Over the years, Wi-Fi has evolved through various standards, including 802.11a, 802.11b, 802.11g, 802.11n (Wi-Fi 4), 802.11ac (Wi-Fi 5), and the most recent 802.11ax (Wi-Fi 6), enhancing speed, range, and overall efficiency.

Wi-Fi Router also known as a Wi-Fi hub, is the device that connects your smartphone, tablet, pc, chromebook or laptop to the internet. The device is usually supplied by your internet service provider and connects to your home phone line.

WiMAX stands for Worldwide Interoperability of Microwave Access and is an implementation of the IEEE 802.16 standard, WiMAX provides metropolitan area network connectivity at speeds of up to 75 Mbit/sec. WiMAX systems can be used to transmit signal as far as 30 miles.

WIMP stands for Windows Icons Mouse Pointer, or sometimes Windows Icons Menus Pointers, and is a term used to describe a user's interaction with a graphical user interface. Windows and MacOS are examples.

Winchester Disk is an early type of disk drive developed by IBM that stored 30MB and had a 30- millisecond access time. It's inventors called it a Winchester in honour of the .30-calibre rifle of the same name. Although modern disk drives are faster and hold more data, the basic technology is the same, so "Winchester" has become synonymous with "hard".

316

Windows 10 is a proprietary operating system developed by Microsoft for tablets, laptops, PCs, and workstations, released as part of its Windows NT family of operating systems. Windows 10 features a graphical user interface with a start menu consisting of various tiles for launching apps, a taskbar showing running apps and an action center for displaying notifications and settings, as well as a file explorer for managing files and folders..

Windows 11 is the successor to Windows 10 and introduces a new user interface along with many other features.

317

Windows Key is the key used in Windows to open the start menu and execute some keyboard shortcuts.

Wireframe is a 3D model constructed from lines and vertices forming a skeletal map of the 3D object. Textures, shading or motion can the be applied to build the finished 3D object. Also referred to as Polygon Mesh.

WLAN stands for Wireless LAN and is a local area network that transmits over the air typically in an unlicensed frequency band such as the 2.4GHz or 5GHz. Wireless access points (called base stations) are connected to an Ethernet switch and transmit a radio frequency over an area of over several hundred feet. See WiFi.

WMF stands for Windows Meta File and is a vector graphics format used mostly for word processing clip art.

Worm is a standalone, self replicating, malicious computer program designed to cause disruption to a network, steal data, install a back door, or even lock files in a ransomware attack.

WPA (Wi-Fi Protected Access) is a security protocol and security certification program developed by the Wi-Fi Alliance to secure wireless computer networks. It was created in response to the weaknesses found in WEP (Wired Equivalent Privacy), the original network security standard for wireless networks. WPA provides stronger encryption by using a temporal key integrity protocol (TKIP) and a pre-shared key (PSK) or Extensible Authentication Protocol (EAP).

WPA2 (Wi-Fi Protected Access 2) is the second generation of Wi-Fi Protected Access security protocol and certification program developed by the Wi-Fi Alliance to secure wireless computer networks. It supersedes WPA (Wi-Fi Protected Access) and is based on the IEEE 802.11i technology standard. WPA2 enhances network security by requiring the use of stronger wireless encryption methods such as AES (Advanced Encryption Standard) and provides two modes of operation:

1. WPA2-Personal (WPA2-PSK), designed for home and small office networks, it uses a pre-shared key (PSK).

2. WPA2-Enterprise (WPA2-EAP), intended for enterprise networks, it uses a RADIUS server for authentication rather than a pre-shared key.

WPA3 (Wi-Fi Protected Access 3) is the latest version of the Wi-Fi Protected Access security protocol and certification program developed by the Wi-Fi Alliance. Introduced to enhance the security features of WPA2, WPA3 provides improved cryptographic strength and more secure authentication methods.

WPS (Wi-Fi Protected Setup) is a network security standard designed to simplify the process of connecting devices to a Wi-Fi network. It allows users to easily set up and add devices to a wireless home network without needing to know the network name (SSID) and password. WPS supports various methods for establishing connections, but the most common ones include pushing a button on the router. While WPS offers convenience, it has been criticized for vulnerabilities that could allow unauthorized access to the network, leading to recommendations for disabling WPS when not in use. Despite its security concerns, WPS remains a feature on many routers to facilitate easy connection for users.

Write Back is data written into the cache by the CPU is not written into main memory until that data line in the cache is to be replaced. Also referred to as Copy Back.

Write Through is a technique for writing data from the CPU simultaneously into the cache and into main memory to assure coherency.

WWW is short for World Wide Web and is a collection of richly formatted graphic/hypermedia documents located on computers around the world and logically linked together by the Internet. With a graphical Web browser users can "surf" the Web by clicking highlighted words on the screen. Each click activates a hypertext link, connecting the user to another Web location identified by a URL.

WYSIWYG stands for What You See Is What You Get and is a screen output that exactly matches the appearance when printed.

WYSIWYG applications such as Microsoft Word or Publisher are common as they allow precise control over formatting and layout without having to worry about what it will look like when printed.

X Y Z

X Windows or X11, is a networked windowing system originally developed at MIT. It provides a graphical user interface (GUI) for UNIX-based operating systems and allows applications to be displayed on remote machines. X11 follows a client-server model, where the X server manages the display, input devices, and rendering, while X clients are the applications that request graphical output..

X10 is a communications protocol for remote control of electrical devices designed for operation over standard household electrical wiring. It transmits data using Amplitude Modulation.

X.25 is an ITU standard for packet-switching networks approved in 1976, X.25 defines layers 1, 2, and 3 in the OSI Reference Model. Such networks are widely used for point of sale (POS) terminals, credit card verifications and automatic teller machine (ATM) transactions. New packet-switched networks employ frame relay and SMDS technologies rather than X.25.

X2 is a technology developed by U.S. Robotics for achieving modem transmissions at close to 56 Kbit/s over ordinary phone lines. See also K56flex.

x64 also known as x86-64, is the 64-bit extension of the x86 instruction set, introduced by AMD as AMD64 and later adopted by Intel as Intel 64. It allows computers to use more than 4GB of RAM, run 64-bit operating systems and applications, and improves performance with additional registers and instruction enhancements.

x86 refers to the family of processors based on the Intel 8086 instruction set architecture (ISA). Originally a 16-bit architecture, it later evolved into 32-bit (IA-32) and 64-bit (x86-64) versions.

x86 processors are widely used in desktops, laptops, and servers, with support for a large variety of operating systems.

xDSL stands for Digital Subscriber Line and is a technology that uses standard copper telephone cables to carry data and shares the same phone line as the telephone service. DSL it uses a different part of the phone line's bandwidth, so it doesn't interfere with normal phone service. This is achieved using a DSL filter. See ADSL, VDSL.

XG is Yamaha's extension of General MIDI that provides many instrument variations and more digital effects. Many instrument parameters can be controlled in real-time.

XGA (Extended Graphics Array) is a graphics standard introduced by IBM in 1990. It supports a resolution of 1024×768 at 256 colors and 640×480 at 16-bit (65,536 colors). XGA was later extended by Super XGA (SXGA) and Ultra XGA (UXGA), but today, the term is commonly used to refer to 1024×768 resolution displays.

XLR is the connector usually found on professional audio and video equipment for transmitting audio signals. Many audio mixing desks have XLR connectors to connect stage mics and instruments.

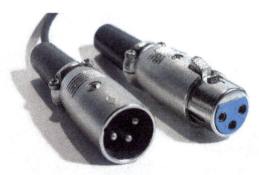

XON/XOFF is a way of controlling the flow of data between a modem and its host computer and between two modems, also called software flow control. XON stands for "Transmitter On" and XOFF stands for "Transmitter Off". If the modem receiving data needs time to process the data or do some other task, it sends an XOFF signal to the host computer (or sending modem). The host computer (or sending modem) then waits until it receives an XON signal before sending more data.

XYZ Planes are the three dimensions of space; each is designated by an axis. The x and y axes are the 2D co-ordinates, at right angles to each other. The z axis adds the third dimension.

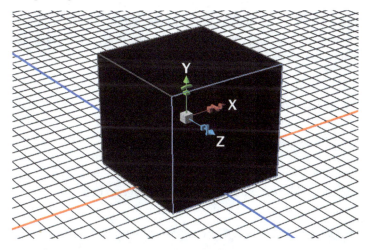

YCrCb is a digital color space used in JPEG compression, MPEG video encoding, and HDTV. Y represents luminance (brightness), while Cr (Chrominance-red) and Cb (Chrominance-blue) carry color difference information. It is commonly used in video compression and digital formats to reduce data size while maintaining image quality.

YIQ is the color encoding scheme used in NTSC (analog television). Y is the luminance (black and white) component, while I and Q are the chrominance (color) components. This method allowed backward compatibility with black-and-white televisions but has been replaced by YCrCb and RGB in modern digital video systems.

YUV is a colour encoding scheme for natural pictures in which luminance and chrominance are separate. The human eye is less sensitive to colour variations than to intensity variations. YUV allows the encoding of luminance (Y) information at full bandwidth and chrominance (UV) information at half bandwidth. YUV is used by the PAL colour system.

Zero Fill is a data-wiping method where storage sectors are overwritten with zeros to erase existing data. This is commonly used in disk formatting, secure data erasure, and SSD preparation. However, data recovery may still be possible, particularly on SSDs due to wear leveling and residual data traces.

ZIF stands for Zero Insertion Force and a type of CPU or IC socket designed to allow the easy installation and removal of components without requiring significant force. Unlike conventional sockets that require direct pressure to insert a processor or chip, a ZIF socket features a locking mechanism, typically a lever or cam, that secures the component in place once it is positioned. This prevents damage to delicate pins and ensures a reliable electrical connection.

ZIF sockets were widely used for Pentium and early AMD processor, however as the technology evolved, ZIF sockets have become less common in consumer electronics. Modern Intel processors now use Land Grid Array (LGA) sockets, where the pins are on the motherboard rather than the processor, while many mobile devices and laptops use Ball Grid Array (BGA) packaging, where the processor is permanently soldered to the board.

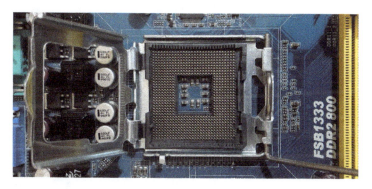

ZIF sockets are also used in Flexible Flat Cable (FFC) and Flexible Printed Circuit (FPC) connectors, which are common in mobile devices, laptops, and other compact electronics. These connectors allow for easy insertion of thin, flexible ribbon cables used in LCD displays, touchscreens, and internal electronic components without risking damage to the fragile conductors.

SOMETHING
NOT COVERED?

We want to create the best possible resources to help you learn and get things done, so if we've missed anything out, then please get in touch using the links below and let us know. Thanks.

---

 office@elluminetpress.com

 elluminetpress.com/feedback